The

Be HEALTHIER
Feel STRONGER
VEGETARIAN
>>> cookbook

The

Be HEALTHIER
Feel STRONGER
VEGETARIAN
>>> cookbook

Susan M. Kleiner, Ph.D., R.D., and

Karen Friedman-Kester, M.S., R.D.

macmillan • usa

MACMILLAN
A Simon & Schuster Macmillan Company
1633 Broadway
New York, NY 10019-6785

MACMILLAN is a registered trademark of Macmillan, Inc.

Library of Congress Cataloging-in-Publication Data

Kleiner, Susan M.
        The be healthier feel stronger vegetarian cookbook / Susan M. Kleiner and
Karen Friedman-Kester.
                p.   cm.
        Includes index.
        ISBN 0-02-861014-8 (alk. paper)
        1. Vegetarian cookery. I. Friedman-Kester, KarenRae. II. Title.
TX837.K554   1997   96-49206
641.5'636—dc21   CIP
ISBN 0-02-861014-8

Manufactured in the United States of America
10 9 8 7 6 5 4 3 2 1

DESIGN BY GEORGE J. MCKEON

To Life!

contents >>

acknowledgments >>

We have had the special privilege to work with and be emotionally supported by many wonderful people. To Justin Schwartz, our editor, thank you for your faith and encouragement. Many thanks to James Park, whose computer and data-entry skills gave us the extra time to spend in the kitchen. Special thanks to the following people for their expertise and assistance and to their institutions for all of their help:

Betty Yuen and Chung Tong of the Bo Loong Restaurant, Nick Cerino, Elaine Friedman, Wayne and Lee Hill, Anjum and Ishrat Jafrie, Mark Shary and Avin Loki Baird of Ke`Ka Restaurant, Randi and Eric Kester, Fabio Midulla, Jim Panushka, Sarah and Christie Thomas, Shelly and Steven Walk, Erika Werne, and Jeff Hamano of the Zojirushi Corporation. We would especially like to thank Mark Kester for his creative suggestions and clever humor.

As always in our lives, we thank Jeff Kanter, Mark Kester, Elaine Friedman, Elinor Kleiner, Leah and Allen Kester, Lee and Wayne Hill, Eric and Randi Kester, Chuck Kleiner and Judy Schuster, and Shelly and Steve Walk for their constant love and support.

preface >>

My first experience with vegetarianism came in 1975 as a college student. The standard dining-hall fare was pretty poor. Word about campus was that there was a vegetarian dining hall that served the most edible food around. But you couldn't switch back and forth between dining halls. Well, the food was decidedly better, and I became a vegetarian overnight.

After several weeks I noticed that I had begun to shed the few extra pounds that I had gained in my first quarter of college — pounds likely due to the higher-fat meat and casseroles that the regular dining hall served. I also found that I really liked all the new foods that I had never tasted before: bulgur, buckwheat, couscous, a variety of beans, and tofu, all prepared in dishes that were new. And lastly, there was a salad bar, great soups, and fresh, steamed vegetables at every meal. I'd always loved vegetables, so I was in heaven. I felt great, I looked great, so being vegetarian was all right with me.

Since college, I have continued with vegetarian-style eating, ranging from total vegan to my present almost-vegetarian diet. I have enjoyed each stage, but have found that both my body and my palate prefer that dairy, eggs, fish, and occasionally chicken, remain in my diet. I have no taste for beef, which is why I don't eat it. And there is no question that plant foods are the foundation of my diet.

But what about you? If you are still on the fence about what to do with your diet, the decision is not all or nothing. The key to health is a plant-based diet, not a meatless diet. If you have no moral or ethical reasons for eliminating animal products from your diet, then don't. There are many important nutrients that we obtain more easily from animal foods than when we rely solely on plant foods. But your health does depend on reducing the amount of meat in your diet to make room for all of the important health-promoting antioxidants, fibers, phytochemicals, and phytoestrogens found only in plant products. And we now know that you can't just get these in a pill. They work best when eaten in their natural combinations found only in food.

If you eliminate animal products from your diet, there is no question that you can stay healthy and strong. But you do need to know what you are doing. The nutrients eliminated by cutting out animal products must be replaced by plant sources, and sometimes by supplementation.

The Be Healthier Feel Stronger Vegetarian Cookbook will give you the latest scientific information about the benefits of a vegetarian lifestyle and how to easily design your diet based on your own personal decisions and philosophies. It is full of tips and cooking techniques to help you create an atmosphere of ease in your kitchen while you prepare the healthiest food for your body. Find out the latest information about which oils to buy, whether organic foods are better, indoor planting and sprouting, food safety, and preserving the nutrients in your food. And of course, enjoy the fabulous recipes that we have created to promote your healthy, high-performance lifestyle.

Some of the fastest and strongest athletes today are vegetarians: Carl Lewis, Al Oerter, and Dave Scott all profess to be vegetarians. Even if you don't plan on becoming an Olympic or Ironman champion, the fact that by following a vegetarian-style diet you will likely live healthier and feel stronger should be convincing enough.

Eat well, live long, and prosper!

—*Dr. Susan M. Kleiner*

I have a secret to share with you. Okay, it's not that much of a secret, but the truth is I'm going to admit it. I'm a carnivore. I like meat! Not just the occasional fish or chicken, but all sorts of meat. I don't eat it every night, but animal products are a part of my diet. As a child, we had meatless meals in our home a number of days of the week. I can't say that they were particularly healthful, as they were usually higher in fat than the meat meals because of all of the added butter and cream. They did have the benefit of adding a variety of vegetables and grains that were not in the diet of mainstream America.

My family's diet was an exception to the classic American diet by having meatless meals. Since the reason for all the meat wasn't health, why did Americans have this meat craze? It sure wasn't the basis of the diet of most immigrants. This national obsession with meat for dinner every night can be traced to President Herbert Hoover and his promise of a chicken in every pot. The truth is, following the Depression, a sign of affluence was eating meat for dinner every night. But meat rationing came in with the onset of World War II. By the end of World War II and the elimination of rationing, our more cosmopolitan society demanded meat nightly.

However, internationally meat did not take on the prominence of the main course as it did in the United States, partially due to the devastation of World War II and the subsequent economic rebuilding, which took decades. Also, the ethnic groups of many European countries were not striving for the assimilation the American melting pot demanded. My grandmothers (from the Old Country) kept their ethnic roots and, for cultural reasons, did not serve meat nightly. My father preferred the more traditional American fare of meat and potatoes and my mother eventually complied. Therefore, as a teenager I got used to meat for dinner nightly, as did many of my contemporaries.

It is only in the last few years, since my husband has hit the big Four-O, that I really pushed to serve meat on an occasional, rather than a daily, basis. The plan I use is to serve vegetarian meals four days a week, usually on weekdays. On Friday, Saturday, and Sunday we eat meat (beef, poultry, and fish) or sometimes we have a vegetarian meal again. The end result is that my husband lost twenty-five pounds in about four months and is healthier. My daughter eats a wide variety of foods, unlike many of her friends who consume a lot of hot dogs and fast foods.

As we began to gather ideas for this book, I searched for unique recipes to provide a variety of dishes that utilized different fruits and vegetables, an assortment of tubers and grains, and a combination of textures and flavors. This generates a matrix of different nutrients and phytochemicals in the diet. I spoke to friends from around the world and gathered their family favorites from Italy, India, Japan, China, Bulgaria, Israel, Russia, and Kurdistan; I visited ethnic restaurants that were willing to share their secrets. The end result is a book that includes a variety of cultures and tastes.

We added a bread section to this book. Bread is a mainstay of diets from around the world and can add depth and texture to many meals. Some recipes are for bread machines and some are to be used in conventional ovens. Either way the smell of fresh-baked bread can set the tone for a delicious and exciting meal. This is the time to get rid of basic white bread and experiment with rye, pumpernickel, whole grain, and other flavorful breads.

Yes, my diet has changed through the years and I wouldn't really call myself a vegetarian, but I am happy to report that eating a healthful, plant-based diet with both vegetarian and occasional meat-containing meals is not difficult and doesn't create feelings of deprivation. Thus, you can eat for healthy living and still eat what you want. However, you can't consume all the vitamins, minerals, phytochemicals, and fiber to prevent disease in one meal. So pick and choose those meals that will have some meat in them and enjoy these vegetarian recipes that we developed to help you eat, feel, and be healthier.

—Karen Friedman-Kester

the be healthier, feel stronger vegetarian diet

As we stand on the threshold of the twenty-first century, nutrition scientists are unraveling a whole new concept: food factors—constituents in foods that are critical to the prevention of chronic disease. Food factors are found primarily in plant foods. But most of us grew up with meat as the centerpiece of our meals. Vegetables, beans, and grains were side dishes—accompaniments to the main meat course. Now research has taught us that eating too much meat means eating too much fat, which can result in the development of chronic diseases like heart disease and cancer. In fact, daily consumers of red meat have a higher risk of colon, prostate, and possibly breast cancer, likely due to the development of certain chemicals during cooking.

The problem is not really that meat is so bad for you—but that grains, beans, nuts, seeds, fruits, and vegetables are so good for you! If you make meat the center of your diet, you just don't have enough room left to eat all the fabulous plant foods necessary to ward off disease. Vegetarian diets have been associated with a lower occurrence of coronary heart disease and cancers of the lung, colon, esophagus, and stomach. And there is now fairly good evidence that a low-fat vegetarian diet can reverse some of the effects of coronary heart disease.

Vegetarian-style diets that are high in carbohydrates and low in fat are the perfect plan for the promotion of physical activity. With 60 to 65 percent of the diet coming from the carbohydrates of grains, beans, fruits, and vegetables, you can use your energy stores to push out the walls of performance. Plant-based, vegetarian-style eating is the diet for the healthy, active body.

HOW TO USE THIS BOOK

It takes time to change from a meat-based to a plant-based style of eating. Even if you are still planning to include some meat in your diet, you are changing the focus of your diet, and you are learning to eat, shop for, and cook new foods, frequent different restaurants, and develop new lifestyle habits that will benefit you for the rest of your life. If you are already almost-vegetarian and are just continuing on a path to which you have already become accustomed, the changes may not seem as dramatic. But if you are just beginning to change your diet, the number of things to concentrate on may seem overwhelming.

To ensure success, make slow, small adjustments to your diet; making rapid, big changes may lead to frustration and dismay. If you are a complete carnivore, start by reducing the amount of meat that you eat, rather than cutting it out of your diet altogether. As long as you are eating lots of grains, beans, fruits, vegetables, nuts, and seeds, small amounts of lean meat in your diet are very healthful. One way to switch from a meat-based to a plant-based style of eating is to plan several vegetarian meals, or vegetarian days, into your diet during the week. This helps you try your new style of eating without the pressure of feeling that you will never be able to eat meat again.

You may choose to stick with an almost-vegetarian meal plan, or you may like to move on to a more vegetarian-based plan. In either case, the recipes that we have created for this book will meet your dietary needs. Once you have planned your diet using the food and nutrient guidelines discussed below, use the delicious recipes to efficiently plan your meals.

Most of the recipes take only thirty minutes to prepare, and all of them take no longer than one hour of hands-on preparation time. All of the recipes are low in fat and high in carbohydrates to meet the demands of a high-performance lifestyle. Each recipe is accompanied by a description of its outstanding nutrient characteristics to help you plan your menus to meet your personal nutritional needs.

The unique calorie and nutrient breakdown that we created for our first book, *The High Performance Cookbook,* is used again here. Everyone has different energy needs, but most active people fall within two categories. People with larger bodies (frequently men), have higher energy needs. To assist with portion control, we have offered two different serving sizes to meet the needs of a higher- and a lower-calorie diet. For a diet close to 3,000 calories a day, use each recipe to yield two servings. If you are very active and need much more than 3,000 calories a day, you might choose to eat a double serving of some of the foods. There are some very high-calorie, low-fat recipes scattered through the book that might also be useful in your diet. For a diet that is closer to 2,000 calories a day, plan on three servings out of each recipe.

Make sure to read Chapter 2, "The Be Healthier, Feel Stronger Vegetarian Kitchen." It will help you outfit your kitchen, plan your shopping, and learn the cooking skills that will help you make the most flavorful and nutritious vegetarian dishes with little effort. By following the guidelines in this chapter, you should be able to walk in the door after work and prepare almost any recipe in the book. It's that easy.

THE BENEFITS OF A VEGETARIAN DIET

FIBER

Without a doubt, a fiber-rich diet is a positive investment in your health. Vegetarian-based diets are richer in both water-soluble and water-insoluble fibers than meat-based diets because fiber is found only in plant foods. It is the structural part of fruits, grains, and other plant foods, the part that humans are unable to digest.

Water-soluble fibers—which come mainly from beans, fruits, and whole grains—have been shown to result in lower blood cholesterol and blood glucose (sugar) levels, beneficial characteristics for the prevention and management of cardiovascular disease and diabetes. Studies have shown that one-half to one cup of beans a day can significantly reduce blood cholesterol levels and help control the blood sugar of diabetics.

Water-insoluble fibers—which come from vegetables, beans, whole wheat, and fruit skins—aid in the normal functioning of the gut, thereby alleviating constipation and diverticular disease, and possibly reducing the risk of bowel cancer.

WEIGHT CONTROL

Dietary fibers have been shown to play an important role in weight-loss diets and overall weight management. Because fiber helps you feel fuller and slows the time that it takes for your stomach to empty, you feel full longer and eat less.

High-fiber diets are lower in calories and are less likely to contribute to the development of obesity. In fact, vegetarians tend to eat less fat and fewer calories than nonvegetarians. Most researchers concur that obesity is a critical factor in the development and progression of cardiovascular disease, cancer, hypertension (high blood pressure), and diabetes. At least partly due to these dietary differences, vegetarians are leaner and suffer far less from these chronic diseases than nonvegetarians. In fact, vegetarians may even live longer than people who eat meat-based diets.

ANTIOXIDANTS

The body's own normal metabolic process called oxidation produces "free radicals," unstable molecules that cause irreversible damage to cell membranes. Fortunately, we have natural systems that protect us from most of the potential damage by disarming the free radicals and alleviating the risks of cell damage. Left unchecked, free radical damage leaves the body vulnerable to advanced aging, cancer, cardiovascular disease, and degenerative diseases like arthritis. The natural chemicals that arm the protective systems are called "antioxidants."

Environmental factors can affect the production of free radicals in the body. For example, cigarette smoke, exhaust fumes, radiation, excessive sunlight, certain drugs, and stress can increase free radical production. When you exercise intensely, your body consumes quantities of oxygen, heats up, produces hormones, and may have some resultant muscle cell damage. These factors also produce an abundance of free radicals.

Numerous substances in our food act as antioxidants or work with the antioxidant systems. Vitamins E and C, and the vitamin A precursor, beta-carotene, have been most widely examined in their relationship with chronic disease prevention and treatment of muscle soreness and damage after exercise. The minerals copper, selenium, manganese, zinc, and iron, and the compound coenzyme Q10 have also been tested.

Cardiovascular Disease One cause of heart disease is arterial plaque, which is the buildup of cholesterol on your artery walls. In 1993, scientists discovered that one cause of this buildup is the oxidation of low-density lipoprotein cholesterol (LDL-C). Through several different mechanisms, the oxidized LDL-C promotes plaque buildup. This narrows the artery and begins the first stage of atherogenesis. Antioxidants prevent LDL-C oxidation and are one way to prevent the buildup of plaque in the arteries.

Early studies of supplements found that the most influential antioxidant affecting LDL-C oxidation is vitamin E, specifically alpha-tocopherol. Studies documenting self-supplementation and risk of heart disease in women and men indicated that the greatest risk reduction occured in the groups that took 100 IU of vitamin E per day. (For ease of understanding, 1 IU of vitamin E=1 mg vitamin E.) More recent research investigating the actual dose response of vitamin E supplementation on LDL-C oxidation found that the minimum dose of alpha-tocopherol needed to significantly decrease the susceptibility of LDL-C to oxidation is 400 IU per day. And there is now preliminary evidence that men already being treated for coronary artery atherosclerosis may benefit from a combined therapy of a cholesterol-lowering diet, drugs, and vitamin E supplementation of at least 100 IU/day.

But just to confuse the issue, a study conducted on 34,486 postmenopausal Iowa women during a seven-year period ending in December 1992, found results that conflict with the studies completed so far. The women who consumed moderate amounts of foods rich in vitamin E had a much lower than average chance of dying of heart disease. Those who avoided such foods had about double the heart disease risk compared to those who ate moderate amounts. But there was no additional benefit for women who took vitamin E supplements.

Cancer   Many population studies have found that when people eat foods that are high in the antioxidants vitamin C and beta-carotene, their risks of developing many types of cancer are diminished. These epidemiological studies have led to study trials investigating whether supplementing with these nutrients in controlled amounts can affect the occurrence and/or progression of various types of cancers, including esophagus, lung, colon, head and neck, breast, mouth, cervix, stomach, and skin.

The jury is still out on many of these studies as we wait for their completion. Some look very promising. However, two studies completed within a year of each other showed such startling preliminary results that the researchers stopped the studies early. In both studies, smokers who took beta-carotene supplements had a greater risk of developing lung cancer than those who did not, just the opposite of what many thought would occur. And in a twelve-year study conducted at Harvard on 22,071 male physicians, no evidence was produced that supplementing with 500 µg of beta-carotene produced any benefit or harm in relation to death from cancer, heart disease, or any other causes.

Antioxidants and Exercise   The most well-tested antioxidants in relation to exercise are vitamins E and C and beta-carotene. The compound coenzyme Q10 has been tested somewhat, and the list of minerals associated with antioxidant enzyme systems remain relatively untested. By far, the most promising data has come from studies investigating the influence of vitamin E on free radical production and oxidative cell membrane damage during, or as a result of, exercise.

During exercise, your body produces more free radicals as a result of increased energy metabolism. This is a natural occurrence. Some investigators have questioned whether our bodies can beef up our antioxidant systems fast enough to respond to the increased free radical production. If not, then greater damage is being done to our cellular membranes, perhaps increasing our risks of early aging and developing chronic diseases.

Another source of free radical production is the damage done to the muscle-cell membrane after intense exercise, especially eccentric exercise, such as putting down a heavy weight or running downhill. This type of training causes a post-exercise muscle injury that results in a secondary production of free radicals that can last for many days. There has been an association between the increased production of free radicals and muscle-cell damage and soreness.

Vitamin E resides in muscle-cell membranes. Part of its job is to scavenge the free radicals produced as a result of exercise, saving the tissues from damage that often occurs. According to a study reported by Dr. William Evans from Penn State University, subjects over the age of fifty-five who participated in an eccentric exercise regimen by running or walking downhill benefited from an 800 IU-per-day vitamin E supplement. Dr. Evans measured neutrophils and creatine kinase, two indicators of the acute repair process that should occur after the muscle-cell damage inflicted by eccentric exercise. When free radicals are not kept in check, this repair process is inhibited, and damage and inflammation continue to occur, even after several days.

The subjects in the study who were younger than thirty responded similarly, whether they were given the vitamin E supplement or a placebo. But in the older group, those who were supplemented with vitamin E responded similarly to the thirty-year-olds. Those given the placebo showed much lower production of neutrophils and creatine kinase, indicating an inhibited repair process.

According to Dr. Evans, this study indicates that vitamin E status and/or function may be compromised as we age, and that supplementation may be prudent. Although this study used 800 IU of vitamin E per day, Dr. Evans believes that 400 IU per day would result in similar benefits.

The bottom line on antioxidants—science marches on, and as is often the case, theories can conflict with one another. When it comes to antioxidants, it seems clear that people who consume diets high in antioxidant-containing foods are protected from the development of many chronic diseases. When the research has been taken into the laboratory, the results appear to be contradictory. Or are they? Perhaps what we are seeing is that the evidence has been somewhat misinterpreted. Instead of using foods as indicators of specific antioxidants, maybe it is the entire food itself that contains the combination of compounds that allow for the protective effect. The antioxidant may be just one factor.

The amounts of vitamin C and beta-carotene that theoretically are protective are easily obtainable from foods, especially if you are eating a plant-based diet. Include a variety of green, orange, and yellow fruits and vegetables as well as plenty of citrus fruits in your diet, and you're there. But getting enough vitamin E in your diet may be tricky because many athletes and health-minded people are lowering dietary fat intakes. Since the greatest sources of vitamin E are foods rich in vegetable oils, such as seeds, nuts, wheat germ, and vegetable oil itself, many diets no longer even meet the Recommended Dietary Allowance for vitamin E (10 mg).

When you base your diet around vegetable foods, it becomes much easier to obtain the recommended levels of vitamin E. Don't be afraid of a little fat in your diet. Although too much fat is not healthful, a diet low in fat does not mean a diet devoid of fat. Remember that vegetable oils are heart healthy. Use a variety of vegetable oils, and eat nuts, seeds, and wheat germ every day to enhance your intake of vitamin E. (See Table 1-1 for best food sources of antioxidants.)

Table 1-1 Best Food Sources of Antioxidants

Beta-carotene suggested daily intake: 3,000–12,000 µg

FOOD	µg BETA-CAROTENE
3 apricots, raw	3,735
½ cup apricots, dried	11,400
1 cup cantaloupe	4,800
½ pink grapefruit	1,611
1 cup mango, sliced	2,145
10 peach halves, dried	12,032
1 cup beet greens, boiled	2,028
½ cup carrots, cooked, canned, frozen	7,154
1 carrot, whole	5,688
1 cup collard greens, cooked	6,912
1 cup kale, cooked	6,110
1 cup lettuce, romaine	1,064

Table 1-1 Best Food Sources of Antioxidants

Beta-carotene suggested daily intake: 3,000–12,000 µg (cont.)

FOOD	µg BETA-CAROTENE
1 cup mustard greens, cooked	3,780
½ cup sweet red bell pepper, raw	1,100
½ cup canned pumpkin, boiled	3,782
1 cup spinach, cooked, drained	9,900
1 cup spinach, raw	2,296
1 sweet potato, baked	10,032
1 cup tomato juice, canned	2,196

Table 1-1 Best Food Sources of Antioxidants

Vitamin C RDA: 60mg; 100mg for smokers

FOOD	MG VITAMIN C
1 cup cantaloupe	68
1 cup black currants	203
1 cup elderberries	52
½ grapefruit	47
1 kiwifruit	57
1 cup mandarin orange, canned	86
1 orange	70
1 cup papaya, sliced	87
1 cup strawberries, fresh	82
1 watermelon slice, 1" × 10"	46
1 cup cranberry juice cocktail	90
1 cup grapefruit juice, from frozen	83
1 cup orange juice, from frozen	97

Table 1-1 Best Food Sources of Antioxidants

Vitamin C RDA: 60mg; 100mg for smokers (cont.)

FOOD	MG VITAMIN C
1 cup vegetable juice cocktail, V8	67
1 cup broccoli pieces, steamed	123
1 cup Brussels sprouts, boiled	97
1 cup kale, boiled, drained	53
1 cup kohlrabi, boiled, drained	89
1 cup snow peas, steamed	84
½ cup sweet red bell pepper, raw	95

Table 1-1 Best Food Sources of Antioxidants

Vitamin E RDA: 10mg men; 8mg women

FOOD	MG VITAMIN E
2 tbsp almond butter	6.3
2 tbsp peanut butter, natural	2.6
2 tbsp sunflower seeds, toasted kernels	9.6
1 tbsp canola oil	3.1
1 tbsp corn oil	2.9
1 tbsp safflower oil	4.7
1 tbsp sunflower oil	8.2
1 cup Complete Bran cereal	10.6
1 cup Corn Total cereal	34.9
1 cup Crispy Wheat 'n Raisins cereal	11.4
1 cup Most cereal	55.0
1 cup Nutrigrain Wheat cereal	11.6
1 cup Product 19 cereal	34.9

Table 1-1 Best Food Sources of Antioxidants

Vitamin E RDA: 10mg men; 8mg women (cont.)

FOOD	MG VITAMIN E
2 tbsp wheat germ, toasted	2.8
1 cup asparagus, steamed	3.6
1 cup beet greens, boiled	2.0
1 cup cabbage, steamed	2.5
1 cup jicama	5.5
1 cup mustard greens, boiled, drained	2.8
1 cup sauerkraut, canned	3.9

PHYTOCHEMICALS

Plant foods contain thousands of phytochemicals. If you are already eating a high-carbohydrate diet, you're probably getting in a reasonable amount of these plant chemicals already. But depending on only high-carbohydrate, starchy foods for your daily dose of phytochemicals may not be enough. Here's why.

Unlike vitamins and minerals, phytochemicals (*phyto* is the Greek word for plant) don't have any nutritive value, but they do seem to protect against cancer, heart disease, and other illnesses. Many of the compounds exert subtle drug-like effects and influence the body's biochemistry in positive ways. Paul Talalay, M.D., director of the Brassica Chemoprotection Laboratory at the Johns Hopkins University School of Medicine, is studying ways for people to mobilize their own cancer-fighting resources through a proper diet. He has already identified a cancer-fighting phytochemical, sulforaphane, in broccoli and hopes to identify more plants with such cancer-fighting powers.

In general, vegetables are a wealth of disease-preventing phytochemicals. Garlic, onions, shallots, leeks, and chives belong to the allium family, which contain organosulfides known as allyl sulfides. Also responsible for making your eyes tear during peeling and preparation, allyl sulfides have been shown in the lab to inhibit tumor production. Studies of human populations have shown that people who eat a lot of garlic and onion have lower risks of cancers of the gastrointestinal tract, such as stomach and colon cancer. Allyl sulfides are found in higher amounts in the most pungent alliums, so that sweet onions like Vidalias and Walla Wallas do not contain as much. Heat can destroy the compounds. But since most of us can't tolerate much raw onion or garlic, a quick saute will retain more allyl sulfides than slow cooking.

Broccoli and cabbage belong to the *Brassica* family of vegetables and contain sulforaphane, indoles, and isothiocyanates. In lab animals, sulforaphane appears to prevent breast cancer. When added to live human cells in a lab dish, sulforaphane activated the production of special enzymes that ward off cancer. Indoles work against dangerously high levels of estrogen, potentially reducing the risk of breast cancer. Isothiocyanates have been associated with prevention of stomach and lung cancers. Cauliflower, Brussels sprouts, and kohlrabi contain sulforaphane and indoles. Watercress, turnips, and Chinese cabbage also contain isothiocyanates.

Carrots, of course, contain one of the most well-known and better-studied phytochemicals—beta-carotene. Responsible for the characteristic orange color of carrots, beta-carotene is an antioxidant nutrient known to thwart the normal metabolic process called oxidation. (For more information about beta-carotene, see previous discussion.)

Tomatoes have as many as 10,000 phytochemicals in them. One of the most important is lycopene, an antioxidant that may help prevent heart disease and cancer. One study indicates that men who eat tomato-based meals at least six times per week have reduced prostate cancer by greater than 60 percent. Other phytochemicals are p-coumaric acid and chlorogenic acid. During digestion, both acids interfere with the production of nitrosamines, which have been implicated in the development of stomach cancer.

Vegetable oils are rich in important phytochemicals. Alpha-linolenic acid, found in vegetable oil, is converted to an omega-3 fatty acid after digestion. Omega-3 fats are inflammation fighters and may help prevent heart disease. And vegetable oils are our greatest natural source of the antioxidant vitamin E.

Condiments and seasonings can contain important phytochemicals also. In addition to cherries, orange peel oil, citrus peel oil, caraway, dill, spearmint, and lemongrass contain a family of chemicals called monoterpenes. Monoterpenes may be associated with a reduction in the risks for cancer of the breast, skin, liver, lung, stomach, and pancreas. Limonene, a phytochemical found mainly in the peel or zest of citrus fruits, with smaller amounts in the fruit itself, helps your liver dispose of cancer-causing agents.

Even beverages contain phytochemicals. Green tea, the light, flavorful tea from the Far East, is being investigated for its anti-cancer properties. Findings point to polyphenols, which work as antioxidants, as protective factors against cancers of the skin, lung, and stomach. The black tea that most Americans drink contains fewer polyphenols than green tea, but research suggests it may also have some cancer-fighting properties.

As a group of phytochemicals, polyphenols are probably found in the greatest abundance. They are in virtually all fresh fruits and veg-etables and in many grains. Polyphenols help protect a plant against the damage caused by ultraviolet light, oxidation, or insects. In addi-tion to the polyphenols found in tea, two other compounds called rutin and quercetin, both widely found in citrus fruits, and a third called curcumin, found in turmeric, are being investigated for their cancer-fighting properties.

PHYTOESTROGENS AND SOY PROTEIN

Another family of phytochemicals are the phytoestrogens, found pre-dominantly in soy-based products like tofu, tempeh, and miso. During a woman's child-bearing years, these natural chemicals help prevent breast cancer by competing with naturally occuring estro-gens in the body. In menopause, estrogen production drops by 60 percent. Phytoestrogens can help make up the difference without increasing the risk of cancer.

Evidence of the power of phytoestrogens can be seen among people who eat plenty of soy foods. Asian women, for example, eat low-fat diets with large amounts of tofu and other soy-based prod-ucts. They have a five times lower rate of breast cancer than women who eat a typical Western diet. When breast cancer does strike Asian women, it takes a more favorable course, with a higher cure rate.

Men needn't feel left out. Because of their regulating action on hormones, phytoestrogens may help prevent prostate cancer, another hormone-dependent cancer. Scientists also feel that some of the phytoestrogens may directly inhibit the growth and spread of hormone-needy cancer cells.

The two most important phytoestrogens now making their mark in this area of nutrition are the isoflavones genistein and daidzen. In test tubes, genistein inhibits the growth of cancer cells but not normal cells. The list of cancer cells thwarted by genistein includes breast, colon, lung, prostrate, skin, and leukemia. And it has just been discovered that isoflavones can be transferred through breast milk to a nursing infant. Research on mice and rats shows that ingestion of isoflavones from breast milk early in life was protective against invading carcinogens and tumors later in life.

Another exciting area of research with phytoestrogens is their role in the defense against heart disease. Phytoestrogens, particularly genistein, found in soy, have been shown to reduce the size of LDL-cholesterol particles (the bad cholesterol) and lower the incidence of coronary artery atherosclerosis in primates.

For decades it has been known that soy protein itself helps to reduce total blood cholesterol levels, LDL-cholesterol, and triglycerides. But it wasn't until recently that a major statistical analysis was done to lend respect to this area of knowledge and motivate health care professionals and nutrition experts to recommend the use of soy protein.

When it comes to consuming soy foods, vegetarians are way ahead of the game. By consuming one-fourth to one-third of your protein in the form of soy (31 to 47 grams per day), you can make a significant impact on your risk of heart disease and cancer. There are many viable sources of soy protein: fresh or canned soybeans, tofu, tempeh, soy milk, and soy milk products such as cheeses and ice creams. But consuming viable, active phytoestrogens isn't quite as simple. We know that there are two types of soy proteins: conjugated and unconjugated. It is the unconjugated form that contains the most bioactive phytoestrogens, and some soy foods do not contain biologically active amounts of phytoestrogens. A study from Tufts University School of Medicine showed that tofu contained high amounts of the active isoflavones genistein and daidzein, but the contents varied slightly between brands. A soy drink contained significantly less isoflavones than the tofu. Soy-based specialty formulas made from isolated soy protein did not contain any phytoestrogens. Textured vegetable protein (TVP), made from soy, also does not contain any active phytoestrogens. But the more traditional soy foods, miso and tempeh, do contain highly bioactive phytoestrogens.

TYPES OF VEGETARIANS

As you can plainly see, there is no way that you can consume all the phytochemicals that have been identified (let alone those that have yet to be discovered) by just popping a pill of dehydrated veggies. The key is to eat a plant-based diet, and there are many strategies for successfully accomplishing this goal.

Over twelve million Americans call themselves vegetarians. But their vegetarian diets fall within a large range of eating styles. For example:

Almost-vegetarians eat dairy foods, eggs, poultry, and fish, but avoid red meat.

Pesco-vegetarians eat dairy foods, eggs, and fish, but no other animal flesh.

Lacto-ovo-vegetarians eat dairy foods and eggs, but exclude animal flesh.

Lacto-vegetarians eat dairy foods, but no eggs or animal flesh.

Ovo-vegetarians eat eggs, but no dairy foods or animal flesh.

Vegans eat no animal foods of any type.

So you see, from almost-vegetarian to pure vegan, any of these styles will offer you the opportunity to expand the amount of plant foods in your diet and still meet your own desires for food and taste.

ENSURING THE PROPER NUTRIENTS

Changing from a meat-centered to a plant-centered diet is not as simple as just eliminating the meat. The trick is to make sure you're not skimping on any nutrients as you cut out certain foods. Vegans run the greatest risk of deficiencies because several vital nutrients are found in significant amounts only in meat, eggs, and dairy products.

VITAMIN B_{12}

One of the most significant nutrients missing from the vegan diet is vitamin B_{12}. Fortunately the body needs very tiny amounts of B_{12}

15

(the RDA is 2.0 micrograms for adults) daily to do its job of helping manufacture red blood cells and nerves. Even so, deficiency is serious, potentially causing irreversible nerve damage.

Eating fermented foods, such as the soybean products miso and tempeh, supplies some vitamin B_{12} from the bacterial culture that causes fermentation, but generally not enough to meet human requirements. Vegans should eat vitamin B_{12}–fortified foods, like fortified soy milk, or take supplements to ensure a healthy diet.

PROTEIN

Protein is the other significant nutrient that must be accommodated for in the vegan diet. All other styles of vegetarian eating include some animal sources of protein. Animal protein contains the nine essential amino acids in the appropriate proportions needed for good health. When this proper configuration of all essential amino acids is available from food, it is called a complete protein. Animal foods are complete protein sources. Plant foods, on the other hand, are termed incomplete protein sources because they may be high in some of the essential amino acids, but low in others.

To get enough essential amino acids from a vegan diet, you have to eat a variety of plant protein sources throughout the day and over a week's time so that those low in an essential amino acid are balanced by one that is higher in the same amino acid. Certain cultures have developed traditional dishes that often combine several foods that complement each other to create complete proteins. Combining beans with grains, flour, nuts, or seeds, such as beans and rice, corn tortillas and refried beans, or pasta and bean soup, creates a fully nutritious protein meal.

As long as your diet includes fish, chicken, eggs, milk, or dairy products, you are eating complete sources of protein. The only catch to the lacto-ovo vegetarian diet is the use of artery-clogging high-fat dairy products. Depend instead on protein-rich plant sources, eggs, low-fat and nonfat milk, cheese, and yogurt.

If you will eat eggs, they are an excellent source of protein. Virtually all the protein in eggs is found in the whites, but the yolk is a good source of iron. Unfortunately, eggs have gotten a bad rap over the years by being branded a cholesterol criminal. But we now know several things about cholesterol and eggs that were not quite so clear when the heart disease–cholesterol connection was first made. The cholesterol in our food plays only a small role in affecting blood cholesterol levels; the real culprit is saturated fats. Research at the Columbia University College of Physicians and Surgeons, looking into whether we really need to limit the number of egg yolks in our diets (because egg yolks contain a significant amount of cholesterol), has found that when subjects followed a low-fat diet, eating two eggs per day had no clinically significant effect on cholesterol levels.

IRON

In absolute amounts, it is surprising to note that most meats are only average sources of iron when compared to many grains and legumes. But the iron that comes from vegetables is not absorbed by our bodies as easily as the iron that comes from animal foods, making meat a valuable source of iron in the diet.

There are two forms of dietary iron, heme iron (from animal tissue like meats, fish, and eggs) and nonheme iron. Absorption of heme iron is affected by the body's own stores of iron, but it is not affected by intestinal factors or by other foods eaten at the same time. However, absorption of nonheme iron is very dependent on iron stores, intestinal factors, and other foods eaten during the same meal. Furthermore, heme iron is absorbed from the intestine at a much greater rate than nonheme iron.

Numerous recent studies have documented a prevalence of iron-deficient conditions in both male and female athletes, but more commonly among women. Non-meat eaters, especially menstruating women and all active people, must pay special attention to their dietary iron needs. (See Table 1-2.)

ZINC

The RDA for zinc is 12mg/day for women and 15mg/day for men. The average zinc intake of both the sedentary and the athletic populations of U.S. women is approximately 10mg/day and that for men slightly more than 15 mg. In a recent study at the University of British Columbia of vegan and lacto-vegetarian women, zinc intakes were lower than recommended (8.5mg/day and 8.2mg/day, respectively).

Excluding meat from the diet may contribute to or increase the potential for the development of low zinc status in athletes. Among the twenty-five major sources of zinc in the U.S. diet, meat or dishes containing meat comprise the top ten. The bioavailability of zinc from some plant sources is limited by their contents and types of fiber. Overall, plant sources of zinc contain lower absolute amounts when compared to animal flesh. So all styles of vegetarian eaters and especially women may be at a greater risk for marginally low intakes of zinc. See Table 1-2 for suggestions on how to meet this nutrient need with a plant-based diet.

Enhance Your Iron and Zinc Absorption

If you have decreased the amount of meat or excluded meat from your diet, you should carefully plan your diet to enhance the availability of iron and zinc. To increase iron and zinc absorption:

Include good sources of iron and zinc in your diet

There are good meatless sources of iron and zinc, as shown in Table 1-2. Don't forget that egg yolks are an excellent source of heme iron. Because your iron and zinc intake may be low or marginal in a completely plant-based diet, an extra effort must be made to include these sources in the diet on a daily basis.

The MFP Factor

Meat, fish, and poultry also contain a special quality called the MFP Factor, which helps the body absorb more nonheme iron. If you do eat some meat, when meat and vegetables are eaten together at the same meal, more nonheme iron is absorbed from the vegetables than if the vegetables had been eaten alone.

Include vitamin C sources

Fruits, vegetables, and other foods that contain vitamin C help the body absorb nonheme iron. For example, if citrus fruits are eaten along with an iron-fortified cereal, more iron will be absorbed from the cereal than if it had been eaten alone.

Avoid iron and zinc absorption-blockers

Some food constituents, called tannins, polyphenols, phytates, and oxalates, can block the intestine's absorption of iron and zinc. Coffee and tea (regular and decaffeinated), whole grains, bran, legumes, and spinach are a few examples of foods that contain iron- and zinc-absorption blockers. These foods are best eaten with heme iron sources and/or vitamin C sources to help the body absorb more iron.

Table 1-2 Good Meatless Sources of Iron and Zinc[1,3]

Breads, Cereals, and Other Grains

FOOD	SERVING SIZE	IRON[2]	ZINC[2]
Bagel, plain, pumpernickel, or whole-wheat bread	1 medium	+	-
Farina, cooked	⅔ cup	++	-
Muffin, bran	1 medium	+	-
Noodles, cooked	1 cup	+	-
Oatmeal, fortified, prepared	⅔ cup	++	-
Pita bread, plain or whole-wheat	1 small	+	-
Pretzel, soft	1	+	-
Ready-to-eat cereals, fortified	1 ounce	++	+
Rice, white, regular or converted, cooked	⅔ cup	+	-
Wheat germ, plain	¼ cup	-	+

Fruits

FOOD	SERVING SIZE	IRON[2]	ZINC[2]
Apricots, dried, cooked, unsweetened	½ cup	+	-

Vegetables

FOOD	SERVING SIZE	IRON[2]	ZINC[2]
Beans, lima, cooked	½ cup	+	-
Spinach, cooked	½ cup	+	-

Table 1-2 Good Meatless Sources of Iron and Zinc[1,3]

Fish and Seafood

FOOD	SERVING SIZE	IRON[2]	ZINC[2]
Carp, baked or broiled	3 ounces	-	+
Clams, steamed, boiled, or canned, drained	3 ounces	+++	-
Crabmeat, steamed	3 ounces	-	+
Lobster, steamed or boiled	3 ounces	-	+
Mackerel, canned, drained	3 ounces	+	-
Mussels, steamed, boiled, poached	3 ounces	+	+
Oysters, baked, broiled, steamed, or canned, undrained	3 ounces	++	+++
Shrimp, broiled, steamed, boiled, or canned, drained	3 ounces	+	-
Trout, baked or broiled	3 ounces	+	-

Legumes

FOOD	SERVING SIZE	IRON[2]	ZINC[2]
Dried beans, cooked	½ cup	+	-
Lentils, cooked	½ cup	+	-
Soybeans, cooked	½ cup	++	-

Nuts and Seeds

FOOD	SERVING SIZE	IRON[2]	ZINC[2]
Pine nuts (pignolias)	2 tbsp	+	-
Pumpkin or squash seeds, hulled, roasted	2 tbsp	+	+

Table 1-2 Good Meatless Sources of Iron and Zinc[1,3]			
Milk, Cheese, and Yogurt			
FOOD	**SERVING SIZE**	**IRON[2]**	**ZINC[2]**
Cheese, ricotta	½ cup	-	+
Yogurt plain or flavored, made with whole or low-fat milk	8 ounces	-	+

[1] Data from USDA (1990)

[2] Servings noted with a + contain at least 1.8mg iron and 1.5mg zinc

Servings noted with a ++ contain at least 4.5mg iron and 3.75mg zinc

Servings noted with a +++ contain at least 7.2mg iron and 6.0mg zinc

[3] Table reprinted from: Kleiner, S.M.: The role of meat in an athlete's diet: Its effect on key macro- and micronutrients. Sports Science Exchange, 1995;8(5)

CALCIUM

Dairy products are our primary sources of calcium. Calcium is essential to health, the formation of bones and teeth, and the lifelong maintenance of bone to prevent osteoporosis. If dairy products are eliminated from the diet, alternative dietary sources of calcium must be included. These include collard, dandelion, turnip, and mustard greens, kale, fortified soy milk, canned fish (because the bones are canned with the fish), beans, broccoli, tofu, and almonds. It still may be difficult to eat enough calcium from vegetable sources, and you might need to consider using a calcium supplement. Talk to your physician and a registered dietitian to help you determine whether you would benefit from calcium supplementation.

In addition to calcium, dairy products are the major source of riboflavin and vitamin D in Western-style diets. Alternative food sources of riboflavin include eggs, whole and enriched grains, brewer's yeast, dark green leafy vegetables, and legumes. Besides getting a little sunshine to help your body manufacture its own vitamin D, including vitamin D–fortified soy milk in your diet will be helpful.

PLANNING A VEGETARIAN DIET

You've now decided to make the switch to some style of a vegetarian diet. Will your exercise performance suffer? What about your energy levels? Can you still develop body-firming muscle even though you're not eating animal protein?

Put your fears aside. Vegetarian diets are typically high in carbohydrates and low in fat. That's the perfect prescription for exercisers and athletes. With 60 to 70 percent of your diet coming from carb-packed grains, beans, fruits, and vegetables, there's no way your performance will drop off. And you can certainly get enough protein to pack on plenty of muscle. But you do have to plan your diet well.

To get enough calories and nutrients, vegetarians should eat at least 1,800 calories a day, with the minimum number of servings from the following food groups:

ALMOST-VEGETARIANS, PESCO-VEGETARIANS, AND LACTO-OVO-VEGETARIANS

6 to 11 servings of bread, cereal, rice, and pasta

3 to 5 servings of vegetables

2 to 4 servings of fruit

2 to 3 servings of milk, yogurt, and cheese

2 to 3 servings of poultry, fish, dried beans, eggs, and nuts

LACTO-VEGETARIANS

8 to 11 servings of bread, cereal, rice, and pasta

3 to 5 servings of vegetables

3 to 4 servings of fruit

2 to 3 servings of milk and yogurt

1 to 2 servings of low-fat cheese

4 to 6 servings of dried beans and peas

2 to 4 servings of nuts and seeds

VEGANS

8 to 11 servings of bread, cereal, rice, and pasta

4 to 6 servings of vegetables

3 to 4 servings of fruit

6 to 8 servings of dried beans and peas

3 to 5 servings of nuts and seeds

Serving size guidelines

FOOD GROUP	SERVING SIZE
Bread, cereals, and other grains	1 slice bread ½ cup cooked cereal, rice, or pasta 1 ounce ready-to-eat cereal ½ bun, bagel, or English muffin 1 small roll, biscuit, or muffin 3 to 4 small or 2 large crackers
Vegetables	½ cup cooked or chopped raw vegetables 1 cup raw, leafy vegetables ½ cup cooked legumes ¾ cup vegetable juice
Fruit	1 medium piece of raw fruit ½ grapefruit 1 melon wedge ½ cup berries ½ cup diced, cooked, or canned fruit ¼ cup dried fruit ¾ cup of fruit juice
Milk	1 cup skim or low-fat milk or yogurt ½ ounce cheese ½ cup cottage cheese
Meat, poultry, fish, eggs, beans, nuts, and seeds	3 ounces cooked lean meat, poultry, or fish 1 egg ½ cup cooked dried beans 2 tbsp peanut butter 1 tbsp nuts or seeds

A GOLD MEDAL LIFETIME

You are now on the road to improving your performance and your life. Many successful athletes have chosen a vegetarian lifestyle. Not only could they perform at peak levels during their athletic careers, but they have maintained good health and longevity throughout the rest of their lives.

Now it's your turn. Never before have we had such an accumulation of scientific knowledge clearly pointing the way to diet and health. Your decision to begin a healthier and stronger vegetarian lifestyle is the best way to support your goals for peak performance now and for the rest of your life.

the be healthier, feel stronger vegetarian kitchen

Cooking has never been so exciting, especially if you love vegetables. Advances in transportation and communication have brought us fruits and vegetables from around the world, and exotic recipes with which to enjoy them. If you've been thinking that eating vegetarian means lots of brown rice and soy patties, think again. People are becoming vegetarian because they love vegetables and want to stay healthy. And they want their meals to look gorgeous and taste wonderful.

When you are busy, planning, shopping, and preparing meals and menus can become a chore. If you are also changing your eating patterns, it may seem overwhelming. Since eating well is a key

25

to achieving peak performance, we've designed this chapter to take the drudgery out of the process and help you enjoy creating your healthier and stronger vegetarian lifestyle.

OUTFITTING YOUR KITCHEN

You can make cooking easy if you have the right utensils and ingredients on hand. With only a few minutes to prepare, you can whip up a dinner for two, including dessert, if you have the right tools at your fingertips, food in the refrigerator, and spices on your rack.

POTS AND PANS

Having the right pots and pans on hand not only eases the task of cooking, but it can make a difference in the nutrient content and quality of the food that you prepare. You'll need a 4-quart pot with a lid for cooking pasta, several smaller saucepans with lids, including one nonstick saucepan with a lid. When it comes to skillets or frying pans, a 10-inch, nonstick skillet with a lid is essential. This can be of a style that can double as a wok, or you can have an additional electric or stove-top nonstick wok. An optional piece of cookware is a cast-iron skillet. When you cook acidic foods (like tomato sauces) in a cast-iron skillet, the acid draws some of the iron out of the cast-iron, and you reap the benefits with a higher iron content in the food.

Other important pieces of cookware include:

One 2-quart oven-safe casserole

Two 1-quart oven-safe casseroles

Two 1-pint oven-safe casseroles

8-inch square microwave-safe and oven-safe pan

Nonstick cookie sheet

Standard-size loaf pan

Oven-safe pie dish

Muffin tin

Double boiler (or two pots that can safely fit one inside the other)

Steamer basket

Nonstick stove-top or electric griddle

KNIVES

Knives are a critical part of the operation in any kitchen. When you are chopping and slicing plenty of vegetables, good knives can make a dull job enjoyable. Remember that a sharp knife is much safer than a dull one. To keep your knives at their best, use a knife sharpener, or take them to be sharpened by a professional. These are the types of knives that we use in our kitchens:

French knife (8 inches)

Serrated knife (two sizes: tomato and bread)

Paring knife

Cleaver (often used for meat, but also an excellent knife for chopping vegetables)

OTHER KITCHEN GADGETS

Considered more as standard equipment than as gadgets, a broiler or gas grill and a microwave oven are really necessary. Among the million and one kitchen gadgets available, we have selected the following essentials:

Blender

Medium-size food processor

Hand-held mixer

Pasta extruder or pasta maker

Colander

Plastic storage containers with lids for storing leftovers and taking food on the road

Kitchen scissors

Vegetable peeler

BREAD MACHINES

With the advent of bread machines, you don't have to love cooking to bake your own bread anymore. If you have never had fresh-baked bread in your house you are missing a real treat. Just the smell is worth the effort. We have included many bread recipes, most designed specifically for the convenience of bread machines. The cost of a machine has become reasonable. A simple bread machine can cost under $100 at many discount stores; more complicated models can range from $300 to $400.

All of the bread-machine recipes in this book were developed on the Zojirushi Home Bakery Bread Machine, a top-of-the-line model. This machine not only mixes the dough and bakes it but can also make cakes and jams. It has numerous settings, from simple dough making to programming your own recipe style.

To choose a machine, look not only at cost but also at issues such as the shape of the loaf (round or square), ease of cleaning and use, and size.

Here's a list of good bread-making tips:

- Know your machine. Some machines require the liquid ingredients to be added first, while others require the dry ingredients be added first. Whatever your machine's directions state is the order you need to add the ingredients, regardless of recipe instructions.

- Note the age of your yeast. Once it has been opened, yeast is only good for about one to two weeks. Older yeast will not allow the bread to rise properly.

- Notice if you are using quick-rising or regular yeast. Use two-thirds the amount of quick-rising yeast than regular yeast.

- Measure your ingredients carefully. With bread machines, precision counts. If your machine instructions state a temperature for water, you need to be right on target or your yeast may not work properly.

If a recipe does not work for your machine, try these remedies:

- If the center of the bread falls in during baking, try reducing the water by 1 tablespoon the next time you make it.

- If the center doesn't bake through also try reducing the liquid, especially if you add moist ingredients like canned fruit.

- If the top of the bread rises too high, reduce your sugar content, check the type of yeast you used, or, if the recipe asked for bread flour and you used all-purpose flour, try reducing the water to compensate for the light flour.

- Climate and altitude also affect your bread. In hot weather or at high altitudes, reduce the amount of yeast.

- Experiment with bread-machine recipes to meet your own machine specifications. Bread machines are finicky. The bread usually tastes fine, but for aesthetics, next time around you can try some of our tips from above. The results are worth it!

IN YOUR PANTRY

Have you ever known someone who can always whip up a great meal on short notice? The secret is having a well-stocked kitchen, starting with the pantry. Nonperishable items that should always be in your cupboard are:

Brown rice and parboiled brown rice

Flavorful white rice such as jasmine or basmati

Bulgur wheat

Couscous

Buckwheat groats

Variety of bread flours

Oatmeal

Assortment of pastas

Variety of nuts and dried fruits

Assortment of oils and vinegars

Variety of dried mushrooms

Sun-dried tomatoes

Variety of dried and canned beans

Tomato paste

Canned whole tomatoes (no added salt)

Low-salt tomato juice

Unsweetened cocoa

Cornstarch

Granulated sugar

Brown sugar

Honey

Molasses

No-stick cooking spray

29

Keep extras of the following items in a cupboard, but always store any opened containers in the refrigerator:

Soy sauce or tamari	Low-fat mayonnaise
Hot sauce such as the Tabasco brand	Unsweetened applesauce
	Pasta sauce
Lemon juice	Pure maple syrup
Barbecue sauce	Low-fat or fat-free salad dressing
Variety of prepared mustards	

If you use oils slowly, buy small bottles and keep them refrigerated to maintain their freshness. (Unsaturated oils, especially monosaturated, can turn rancid if not refrigerated.)

HERBS AND SPICES

Using the right herbs and spices is critical to making delicious foods, especially with vegetarian cooking. It is often preferable to use a fresh rather than a dried herb. If you are substituting a dried herb for a fresh one in a recipe, use about one-third less than the amount of the fresh herb called for. Also, herbs and spices do not stay fresh forever. If you've had bottles of dried spices for longer than one year, do your tastebuds a favor and replace them.

Always have the following spices on hand:

Allspice	Cumin
Basil	Dillweed
Bay leaves	Marjoram
Black peppercorns	Mustard seed (yellow)
Cardamom seeds	Nutmeg
Chili powder	Oregano
Cinnamon	Paprika (mild variety)
Cloves	Red cayenne pepper
Crushed red pepper	Rosemary

Salt   Thyme

Salt-free herb/vegetable   White pepper
seasoning mix

IN AND AROUND THE FRIDGE

Maintaining a vegetarian kitchen means always having a stock of staple vegetables. In a cool spot in the kitchen (but outside the refrigerator), keep a variety of onions, potatoes, sweet potatoes, yams, parsnips, and winter squashes. Fresh garlic can be stored in a garlic keeper in the refrigerator or in a basket in a cool place in the kitchen.

In the refrigerator, have a variety of fresh and frozen green, yellow, and orange vegetables. Choose among fresh and frozen to suit your own lifestyle. You don't want fresh vegetables getting limp or moldy. If you don't use the fresh vegetables fast enough, choose frozen instead. Great items to have are precut fresh and frozen vegetables for salads and stir-fries. Carrots, scallions, and fresh herbs and seasonings like basil, cilantro, ginger, and parsley are a must.

Other ingredients that are used frequently in our recipes and that will be very useful to have at anytime are eggs, tofu, a variety of fresh and frozen fruits, and nonfat or low-fat dairy products like plain yogurt, sour cream, milk, cottage cheese, ricotta cheese, Parmesan cheese, and various shredded low-fat and fat-free cheeses. Shredded cheeses and grated Parmesan cheese can be kept in the freezer to extend freshness and still work great in recipes.

We call for low-fat tofu in all of our tofu recipes. Unfortunately, low-fat tofu may not be available in all areas. If available, we recommend the Mori Nu brand, or if it is not available, select your regional brand. Although tofu is an inherently healthful food, the fat content of regular tofu is about double that of the low-fat kind. Depending on whether you use regular or low-fat tofu, the nutrient breakdown of the given recipe will change by about 4 grams.

Frozen legumes are a wonderful convenience food. They are already cooked, but they're not as soft as canned legumes. Look for lima beans, butter beans, black-eyed peas, and others in the frozen foods section of your supermarket. Keep a selection in your freezer for a fast and easy bean soup or burrito.

31

STORAGE TIPS AND GUIDELINES

Storing your fruits, vegetables, spices, and herbs correctly will make a huge difference in how long they stay fresh and how well they taste. Some things store best when refrigerated. Others, like tomatoes, lose their flavor when refrigerated. And don't store onions with potatoes. The potatoes give off moisture that leads to spoilage.

When buying greens and herbs, start with the best quality that you can find. They should be vibrant, crisp, and blemish free. Stems or core ends should look freshly cut rather than dried out, wilted, or discolored. Get them ready for storage by removing elastic bands or twist ties. Don't wash or cut greens or herbs until you are ready to use them, but pull off yellowed leaves and pat them dry. Place them in a perforated plastic bag and store in the coldest, moistest part of the refrigerator—usually the bottom crisper drawer.

Sturdy herbs, like parsley, thyme, or oregano, can be stored like greens in the refrigerator. Fragile herbs like basil, cilantro, and chervil should be placed in a glass of water (like a flower bouquet) and covered loosely with a plastic bag. Do not refrigerate them, as they deteriorate quickly when chilled.

Since fruit is generally shipped unripe during most of the year, it needs to stay out of the refrigerator until it ripens and then be refrigerated. To speed ripening, place fruit in a closed paper bag on a kitchen counter. The gases produced by the fruit promote the ripening process. Check it daily so it doesn't overripen.

If you purchase fresh tofu (sold loose in water), or don't use a whole brick at once, you must store it properly to save freshness. Tofu should be covered in water (change daily) and stored in the refrigerator.

By handling tofu in different ways, its texture can be altered to create new recipes. Pressing tofu makes it drier, best for dishes that get mixed a lot, like stews or stir-fries. Press tofu by placing a brick in a pie plate or other shallow container. Stack another plate directly on top and weigh it down with something slightly heavy, like a half-filled tea pot or two cans of food. Let it sit for 15 to 20 minutes. Pour off the water and repeat the pressing. For an even firmer, drier tofu, repeat again.

Freezing tofu (it can be frozen for up to three months) is a good technique for making a chewier and more absorbent product that also works well in stews, stir-fries, and marinades. Drain and press a brick of firm or extra-firm tofu. Cut it into cubes or rectangles, and place the cubes in a covered container and freeze at least overnight. Don't worry about the yellowish color of the frozen tofu. It will return to its original color when thawed.

To thaw tofu, place it directly into a bowl of hot tap water for 20 to 30 minutes. Remove the tofu when thawed throughout. Gently squeeze out the water and continue to use in cooking. If you plan to use tofu in a blended recipe, do not freeze it.

Table 2-1: Where to Store Fruits and Vegetables

FOOD	REFRIGERATED	UNREFRIGERATED
Root vegetables potatoes, yams, turnips, parsnips, onions		X (and away from light and heat)
Spring/summer onions green onions, sweet onions	X	
Winter squash		X
Tomatoes		X
Other vegetables celery, carrrots, etc.	X	
Mushrooms	X (in mushroom keeper or dry paper)	
Garlic	X (in garlic keeper)	X (cool, dry place)
Ginger	X (in rice wine)	X (cool, dry place)
Dried herbs and spices		X (away from light and heat)
Unripe fruit		X
Ripe fruit	X	
Bananas		X

There are lots of little tips and tricks to handling fruits and vegetables that will increase their aesthetic appeal and their taste. You may have wondered why chefs take the time to break up lettuce leaves by hand rather than just cutting them into pieces. When the metal from knives touches the lettuce, it can lead to rusting, or browning. By breaking the lettuce, you avoid this unpleasant result.

Other types of produce turn brown when handled in certain ways. Bananas, apples, and pears brown very quickly after being opened and sliced, so that serving them in fruit salads can be unappetizing. Avoid this by dipping the cut surfaces of the fruit in a mixture of lemon or orange juice and water. The acid will alleviate the oxidative process that results in browning.

Root vegetables like potatoes also brown soon after peeling. As you cut up the potatoes, immediately place them into a bowl of cold water to halt the browning process. Make sure to cook them right away. Soaking for any length of time will cause a leaching of the water-soluble nutrients and a loss of nutrient value from the food.

Most cooks have a trick for cutting onions without crying. One remedy is to stick your head in the freezer when you feel tears coming on and breathe deeply. Another more effective tactic is to chill the onions before cutting them for at least 30 minutes. You can remove the odor of onions from your hands by rubbing them with lemon juice or salt.

If you've never worked with dried mushrooms before, you will have a chance with a few of our recipes to experiment with these great delicacies. Before rehydrating them, discard the stems and any other part that is yellow or yellowish green. This coloring is an indication of spore growth. After rehydrating, discard any parts that do not soften.

FOOD SAFETY

You might think that by eliminating meat from your diet, you have automatically eliminated the major culprit in the cause of food poisoning. Not true. You can get food poisoning from any food: meat, fruit, fish, or vegetable, and the major cause is the way the food has been handled by the preparer—that is, poor sanitation (unwashed hands). This person can be you!

In addition to washing your hands before you prepare any kind of food, you should always follow several other food handling and safety guidelines.

GUIDELINES

- Wash all fruits and vegetables thoroughly.

- Store partially used canned goods, including juices, in glass or plastic containers.

- Keep hot foods hot and cold foods cold. The Danger Zone of 60°F to 125°F allows rapid growth of bacteria and production of toxins. Do not hold foods in this temperature zone for more than 2 to 3 hours.

- Throw out foods that show signs of mold. Even though you might not see the mold throughout the food, parts of the growing mold may be invisible to the naked eye.

- Handle eggs safely. Buy clean, sound, odor-free, fresh eggs that have been refrigerated. Throw out any cracked or broken eggs.

- Keep eggs refrigerated. They will stay fresh for 4 to 5 weeks at 45°F.

- Refrigerate eggs in the cases in which you purchased them to avoid unnecessary handling and to insulate them from any odors of food nearby.

- Cook eggs thoroughly. Keep cold egg dishes colder than 40°F and hot egg dishes hotter than 140°F.

- Before and after handling, clean and wash everything that comes into contact with eggs, especially raw ones. That includes your hands, mixing bowls, utensils, pots, and pans.

NUTRIENT PRESERVATION

There are some basic principles to preserving the nutrients in food, especially for those in fruits and vegetables. Some nutrients, like certain vitamins, are sensitive to heat, light, water, and oxygen. Others, like minerals, are not. Once a fruit or vegetable is picked, the nutrient composition of that food begins to change. We can minimize the loss of nutrients from our food by following some very simple guidelines.

GUIDELINES

- Always purchase fresh produce.

- Store produce in its whole form, rather than cutting it up.

- Never soak produce for extended periods of time.

- When peeling and paring, remove as little as possible.

- If you purchase precut produce, refrigerate it in air tight wrappers or containers.

- Cook vegetables in large pieces to lessen the amount of exposed surface to water.

- Bring cooking water to a boil before adding vegetables.

- When boiling vegetables, return the water to a boil as quickly as possible.

- Cook in just enough water to prevent scorching and put a lid on the pan. (Do not cover vegetables such as broccoli, Brussels sprouts, cabbage, and cauliflower because the color and flavor will suffer.)

- Cook the vegetables only until tender, yet still slightly crisp, and serve promptly.

Microwaving

One way to preserve the nutrients in your food is to use a microwave. Defrosting foods in the microwave is fast and easy, and it eliminates the time that the food sits in water, losing precious water-soluble nutrients.

Since microwaving requires little water, many nutrients are preserved. Nevertheless, we prefer many vegetables steamed the old-fashioned way because they are more tender. The quality of the product is just not the same.

On the other hand, we definitely recommend microwaving for reheating foods, cooking spaghetti squash, rehydrating dried fruit, dried mushrooms, and sun-dried tomatoes, and melting chocolate and butter. Potatoes, yams, and winter squashes that are going to be used as cooked ingredients in other recipes do well in the microwave. And if you are in a time crunch, microwaving them to eat as is will do. But if you have the time, potatoes, yams, and winter squash come out much fluffier when cooked in a conventional oven.

If you are going to purchase a microwave, make sure to get one with a rotating dish. This allows for the most even distribution of the waves during cooking, without stopping the cooking process several times to turn your food. Many of the ovens come with lots of bells and whistles. Unless you become the "microwave maven," it is unlikely that you will ever use most of these extras. So don't pay the extra dollars to buy them.

MAKING YOUR OWN SOUP STOCK

There are several different ways to make soup stock; we've included two recipes in the recipe section of the book. Making your own soup stock need not be difficult or time-consuming. Once you have mastered the basic theory you can create your own delicious soups in minutes. Soup leftovers can be frozen, refrigerated for up to one week, or turned into other soups or casseroles.

The easiest way to make your own soup stock is to save the water in which vegetables have been cooked, and combine it in a jar or covered crock in the refrigerator. Don't use the cooking water from vegetables like broccoli, cauliflower, Brussels sprouts, and cabbage; the high sulfur content of these can make a bitter-tasting broth.

Another method is to take all the odds and ends of all the vegetable trimmings that you have from other recipes, add water, and boil them down for an hour or so. This stock will keep in a covered jar or crock in the refrigerator for about one week.

One way to extend the life of a stock is to reduce it by simmering on low heat, uncovered, until half the liquid has evaporated. Pour the cooled liquid into ice cube trays and freeze. You can use individual cubes for recipes that call for broth or stock on a one-to-one basis.

BEAN MUSIC

Most people have some gastrointestinal reaction to beans.

A small amount of the carbohydrate in beans is from sugars, including raffinose, stachyose, and verbacose. These sugars are at the root of most of the intestinal problems attributed to beans. Our gut does not contain the enzymes required to digest these sugars in the small intestine, and so they arrive in the large intestine undigested. Bacteria that live in the large intestine have a heyday feeding off and fermenting these sugars, producing carbon dioxide, hydrogen, and a few other gases (a.k.a. flatulence) as by-products.

But there is a way to reduce 60 percent of the gas-producing problem by following these easy steps:

Soak dried beans for 4 to 5 hours (or overnight, or from the time you leave for work in the morning until you return home in the evening); discard the water.

Add fresh water, bring beans to a boil for 10 minutes, reduce the heat to medium-low, and cook for half an hour or until tender, and again discard the water. For best results, add 9 cups of water for every cup of beans.

If the beans still require cooking, add more water, simmer, and discard this water as well. Most beans require approximately 1 to 2 hours of cooking.

Some of the gas associated with eating beans is due simply to increasing the fiber content of your diet. By increasing the fiber content slowly, your body will ultimately adapt to the change and your discomfort will diminish. Any remaining discomfort caused by residual undigested sugars can be relieved by using the product Beano (AkPharma Inc.), available in most supermarkets, natural-food stores, and pharmacies. Beano is an enzyme preparation that will help you digest undigestible sugars.

OVERTURE TO OILS

Cooking with a variety of oils plays an important role in creating flavorful vegetarian fare. Not only do they add flavor, but different oils offer your diet an array of important nutrients as well. (See Table 1-1.)

Your be healthier, feel stronger vegetarian diet is designed to be low in fat. But that is not the whole story. The type of fat that you have in your diet is equally important. Saturated fats and hydrogenated fats have been closely linked with the development of high blood cholesterol levels and increased risks of heart disease. Monounsaturated and polyunsaturated fats have been shown to be helpful in decreasing the risks of developing heart disease. So, built in to your plan is the healthful strategy of eating a diet that is higher in monounsaturated fat, moderate in polyunsaturated fat, and lowest in saturated fat.

Although no oil falls into a single category, each is categorized into predominantly polyunsaturated or monounsaturated types. Saturated fats generally are solid fats. Those that become cloudy in the refrigerator, like olive, canola, peanut, and sesame oils, are mainly monounsaturated. Polyunsaturated oils like corn, safflower, sunflower, walnut, and hazelnut remain clear and stay liquid in the refrigerator.

Oils can also be classified by the method used to extract them from their original source. Cold-pressing retains more flavor and slightly more nutrients than extracting oils by heat or chemicals.

Overall, oils are more healthful than solid fats like butter and shortening. But oils and solid fats have different physical properties, and one cannot always be substituted for the other in cooking. In baking, for instance, butter and shortening allow for the development of a flaky, crispy product. If a recipe requires melted butter, oil may be substituted, but the final product will be chewy, rather than light and crispy. And in many cases, oil cannot reproduce the flavor of butter in a recipe.

As long as healthful sources of oil, such as nuts and seeds, and vegetable oils themselves, are the predominant sources of fat in your diet, you may add a little butter to vary flavors and textures in a vegetarian diet. And it certainly will not compromise your health. Several recipes in this book use small amounts of butter because nothing else works quite as well. If you have chosen to eat a diet without dairy foods, it is unlikely that replacing the butter with oil in the recipe will be successful. We suggest that you skip that recipe and go on to one without butter. After all, if it doesn't taste great, why eat it?

ORGANIC FOODS

Have you ever wondered about what's on your food that you can't see? Most people who are interested in health and fitness have questioned the use of fungicides, herbicides, and insecticides, otherwise known as pesticides, in and on the food they eat. Despite assurances from the government that the United States has the safest food supply in the world, health-conscious consumers are demanding more purity in their foods. This consumer demand has turned the production of organic foods into a $3 billion industry, and organic foods are more widely available than ever before. But are organic foods better?

WHAT DOES "ORGANICALLY GROWN" MEAN?

The term "organic" does not have a functioning federal definition. In 1990, Congress passed a law defining a federal standard for organic farming methods. The bill has not been implemented yet, but it is slated to be in place for the 1997 growing season.

At present, the job of regulating the organic farming industry is left up to each state on a volunteer basis. Enforcement and oversight varies from state to state, and not all states have instituted organic programs or statute definitions. In general, organically grown foods are:

• Grown in soil enriched with organic fertilizers rather than synthetic fertilizers.

• Treated only with nonsynthetic pesticides.

• Grown using a soil-building program that promotes vibrant soil and healthy plants, usually including crop rotations and biological pest control.

WHAT ARE THE REAL RISKS?

The use of pesticides for growing food is highly regulated. New pesticides are strictly tested over many years. The Environmental Protection Agency must decide both that the pesticide causes no unreasonable adverse effects to people and the environment and that benefits outweigh the risks of using it. However, there is concern about older chemicals registered before 1970, when less stringent testing conditions were permitted.

The actual risk of poisoning from exposure to pesticides in food depends on the potency of the chemical; its concentration in food; how much and how frequently it is eaten; and an individual's resistance or susceptibility to the substance. Increased rates of several types of cancers in humans have been linked to higher-than-average uses of pesticides. But the levels of pesticide residues found in foods are almost always well below the tolerance levels that have been set to meet safety concerns.

Produce that is imported from outside the United States may be tainted with illegal chemicals. In general, it is stopped at the border by Food and Drug Administration (FDA) testing. But with six hundred pesticides available on international markets, many are not detectable by the FDA. This has raised concerns among pesticide critics with regard to imported foods.

Are Children at Greater Risk?

In recent years, children have been the lightning rod for criticism of the use of pesticides on the nation's food supply. Children face a higher risk from pesticides than do adults for several reasons.

- Since children eat more food than adults do in proportion to their body weight, their exposure to pesticides is greater.

- Children eat more fruit compared to adults, hence consuming more foods that are potential sources of pesticide residues.

- Children will often focus on one or two foods in their diet, and eat much of that food. If that food has pesticide residues, it will increase their exposure to pesticides.

- Since most residues are fat soluble and they accumulate to toxic levels over a long period, exposure at an early age carries a greater risk than does exposure later in life.

- Cells in children are rapidly dividing and enzyme systems to detoxify chemicals may not be fully developed, resulting in a greater susceptibility to the effects of carcinogens and neuro-toxins in pesticides.

Are Organic Foods Better?

Advocates of organic foods claim that such foods are more nutritious, with fewer health hazards associated with pesticide contamination. In general, this argument does not seem to hold up.

Some surveys find similar pesticide levels in both organically and conventionally grown foods. Even when organic foods are grown according to certification standards, run-off water, soil shifting, and pesticides floating in the air may still result in pesticides being present on food.

Organically grown food does not have greater nutritive value than food grown with conventional methods. The soil nutrients from natural fertilizers are no different than the nutrients in chemical fertilizers made in factories. The genetic makeup of the food will also determine a plant's nutrient content and needs.

The freshness of organic foods can also be questioned. Because in many states an efficient production, distribution, and retail sales system is not in place for organic produce, the slow movement from field to market may cause wilting and nutrient losses.

Organically grown produce costs much more than its conventional counterparts. Depending on the supply and demand, this difference can be quite significant.

Human and Environmental Safety

According to Miles McEvoy, program manager for the Washington State Department of Agriculture Organic Food Program, organic foods are not safer and they are not better. His reasoning for promoting organic farming is that it is "a more environmentally benign way of producing food."

The use of pesticides helps to ensure the survival of some crops. But there is some question as to whether the widespread use of pesticides has really improved the overall yield of food. American agriculture uses ten times more insecticide today than forty years ago, and insects are destroying more crops today than ever before.

Herbicides, insecticides, and fungicides persist in the environment for many years and may cause permanent damage to the air, land, and water. High doses of pesticides cause severe health defects in laboratory animals. Ground water run-off from farms can cause contamination of waterways, placing wildlife at risk. The National Academy of Sciences has urged a decrease in the use of chemical agricultural techniques.

Many pesticides are broad-spectrum poisons that damage all living cells, not just those of pests. Those people who handle the chemicals in concentrated form, from manufacturing to application, are at risk. Farm workers can be poisoned during pesticide transport and application. In the mid-1980s, a massive pesticide leak from a factory in Bhopal, India, killed at least three thousand people.

Organic farming methods are less harmful to the environment. For one, the use of natural products helps to improve the soil. Organic pest control generally relies on preventative measures such as crop rotation and biological controls. These place little to no stress on the earth or its wildlife inhabitants.

The Bottom Line

In the end, the choice is yours. The purchasing of organic foods is not just a nutritional issue, but a political and social issue as well. Nutritionally speaking, it is clearly most important to eat a variety of foods to ensure a balanced nutrient intake and to lessen pesticide contamination from any one source. In spite of the use of pesticides, populations that eat large amounts of fruits and vegetables have lower rates of cancer.

You will usually pay more for organic produce. So if your pocketbook is light, buy fresh, conventional produce and follow the guidelines for reducing pesticide residues in foods. If you choose organic, shop on the days that produce is delivered in order to buy the freshest, highest quality food.

If Mother Earth had her say, which do you think she would choose?

GUIDELINES FOR REDUCING PESTICIDE RESIDUES IN PRODUCE

- Wash fresh produce with a scrub brush and rinse thoroughly under running water.

- Use a knife to peel an orange or grapefruit; do not bite into the peel.

- Discard the outer leaves of leafy vegetables such as cabbage and lettuce.

- Peel waxed fruit and vegetables; waxes don't wash off and can seal in pesticide residues.

- Peel vegetables such as carrots, and fruits such as apples, when appropriate. (Peeling removes pesticides that remain in or on the peel, but also removes fibers, vitamins, and minerals.)

INDOOR GARDENING AND SPROUTING

Growing an indoor garden can add beauty to your home and pleasure to your tastebuds. Lots of veggies can be grown in containers indoors. Some of the easiest to cultivate are the miniature and dwarf varieties of radishes, lettuce, and other greens, bush beans, peas, and cucumbers that have compact plants and are well suited to potting. They also take up the least amount of space and have excellent yields.

Herbs are a great starting place for the novice indoor gardener. They are usually easy to grow, and the results are quick in coming. You'll always have fresh herbs for your recipes, and you'll appreciate the low impact that home-grown herbs have on your wallet.

There are many books about container gardening. Your local garden center should also be able to get you started with some soil, seed, or seedlings. You provide the water, sunshine, and tender loving care.

By far the simplest way to "grow your own" is to sprout seeds, grains, or beans—the easiest to grow are alfalfa seeds and mung beans. There is a wide variety of sprouting seeds and beans available in most natural food stores. When you go shopping for sprouting seeds, you'll probably also find several sprouting systems for sale, such as wide-mouth jars with specially designed lids for draining, or even stackable sprouting trays. These are all good systems, but you can also make your own very simple system that works just as well. For instance, instead of specially made covers for the jars, use cheesecloth, wire mesh, or two layers of clean nylon stocking.

To begin sprouting, soak the seeds or beans overnight and then drain off the water. Put them in a wide-mouth jar covered with one of the above items. Put the jar on its side in a dark, warm place (covering with a towel will suffice). Keep the seeds moist but not wet, by rinsing twice a day with lukewarm water and swishing gently. Be sure to drain the water thoroughly because too-moist seeds can rot.

In three to five days (depending on the seeds), the sprouts will be ready to eat. Put them in the sun for several hours to gain vitamins and chlorophyll. Because they are extremely delicate, sprouts from most seeds should be eaten only raw or as a garnish on hot dishes. Bean sprouts are hardier and can be cooked.

EXOTIC FOODS IN THE VEGETARIAN DIET

Most of the recipes in this cookbook use ingredients that are readily available in any supermarket nationwide. But because vegetarian-style cooking is popular internationally, we've included some recipes from around the world that use ingredients that you may need to buy in specialty food stores. Here is a small list of some of the ingredients you might find in our recipes, with accompanying descriptions.

Choley: A white garbanzo bean found in Middle Eastern and Indian cuisines. Usually purchased as a dried bean, this can be found in international, Middle Eastern, or Indian food stores.

Edamame: Fresh, green soybeans in the shell. These are only available seasonally, so they are most often found frozen in Asian food markets.

Hoisin Sauce: A Chinese sweet, barbeque-style sauce made predominantly from soybeans, sugar, molasses, salt, water, and spices. Hoisin sauce is available at well-stocked supermarkets, Asian markets, and natural food stores.

Miso: A rich, salty paste made from soybeans and a grain, such as rice or barley, salt, and a mold culture. Miso is aged in wooden vats for one to three years. The flavor of miso ranges from delicate to mellow and somewhat sweet to savory and salty, with complex flavors. Colors range from the delicately flavored light tan to the more savory and salty dark brown. Miso contains vitamin B_{12} as a by-product of the metabolism from the mold culture. Miso is generally available at Asian and natural food stores.

Plum Sauce: A Chinese sauce made from plums, honey, rice vinegar, soy sauce, vegetable oil, ginger, and chili pepper. It is traditionally used in stir-fries, noodle dishes, and barbeques. It is available in many supermarkets, Asian markets, and natural food stores.

Seitan: Wheat gluten, the elastic protein remaining after starch is rinsed out of flour dough, is used as a meat substitute in vegetarian cooking. It can be purchased already seasoned in many natural food stores.

Sivanyiyan or Shairyan: A fine wheat noodle often used in cuisines associated with Islamic culture, it can be purchased in any Indian or Middle Eastern food store.

Soy Sauce: A dark brown, salty-tasting liquid made from fermented soybeans and used in many Asian cuisines. Poorer-quality products are made with corn syrup, caramel color, and preservatives. Look for shoyu soy sauce made from water, soybeans, sea salt, and whole wheat, or tamari soy sauce, made without wheat. These are available at many supermarkets, as well as Asian and natural food stores.

Tempeh: Pronounced "TEM pay," this chunky cake is originally from Indonesia and is made from cooked whole soybeans fermented with a bacterial culture. Like miso, this bacterial culture beneficially contaminates the tempeh with vitamin B_{12}. Tempeh has a nutty taste and a firm, chewy texture. It is available in some well-stocked supermarkets, as well as Asian and international food markets, and natural food stores.

Tofu: Also known as bean curd, this is made by combining fresh hot soy milk with a curdling agent. There are many different styles available, including soft, firm, extra firm, and silken, in regular and low-fat versions. Each style has different properties, is popular in different cultural dishes, and works best in different recipes. Soft and firm tofu are best used for spreads; firm and extra firm are most useful when the tofu needs to retain its shape. Silken tofu is often used in desserts, like puddings and pies. Today, tofu is generally available at most supermarkets nationwide.

There is nothing like fresh tofu. The flavor is completely different than boxed tofu. Fresh tofu is delicious eaten raw with a little hoisin sauce. For a variety of styles, or to find freshly made tofu, visit an Asian market.

Wonton Skins: Also known as "Asian wrappers," these can be found thin, best used for steaming; medium, best used for steaming or frying; and thick, best used for frying. Wonton skins should be stored in a refrigerator or freezer for up to six months. At least one type of thickness is available at most supermarkets, but Asian markets offer a better selection.

amazing
appetizers
and sensual
sauces

bean dip >>

Beans are great energy for that get-up-and-go feeling. This dip makes an easy packable lunch for work or trailside.

*For **2 servings** each serving contains:*

Calories:	272
Fat:	2g
Protein:	18g
Cholesterol:	1mg
Carbohydrates:	45g
Sodium:	1619mg

*For **3 servings** each serving contains:*

Calories:	181
Fat:	2g
Protein:	12g
Cholesterol:	1mg
Carbohydrates:	30g
Sodium:	1079mg

2 cups canned pinto beans, drained

½ cup chopped fresh seeded tomatoes (drain off excess liquid)

½ cup nonfat yogurt, drained

½ tablespoon minced chives

1 teaspoon salt

½ teaspoon freshly ground black pepper

½ chili, seeded, such as jalapeño or serrano

¼ cup fresh cilantro

1. Place all the ingredients into a food processor and process until smooth.

2. Serve chilled with tortillas.

bean tapenade >>

The trendy culinary rage of the '90s is tapas and tapenade. Tapas are Spanish appetizers. A tapenade is a spread or paté. It is often served in Spanish restaurants as part of the tapas bar offerings.

One 14-ounce can white beans, drained

1 tablespoon grated lemon zest

1 tablespoon extra virgin olive oil

1 tablespoon minced garlic

1 tablespoon fresh sage, minced

Salt and freshly ground black pepper to taste

2 rolls, sliced into small rounds

1. Combine all the ingredients except the rolls in a food processor and process until smooth.

2. Serve the spread on the sliced rolls.

nutrition info

*For **2 servings** each serving contains:*

Calories:	691
Fat:	11g
Protein:	27g
Cholesterol:	0mg
Carbohydrates:	120g
Sodium:	794mg

*For **3 servings** each serving contains:*

Calories:	461
Fat:	8g
Protein:	18g
Cholesterol:	0mg
Carbohydrates:	80g
Sodium:	529mg

49

baked onion >>

You won't be shedding tears with this low-calorie appetizer. It is high in nutrient density and full of vitamins, minerals, and phytochemicals. It goes great with a hearty bowl of soup and a salad.

nutrition info

*For **2 servings** each serving contains:*

Calories:	269
Fat:	10g
Protein:	7g
Cholesterol:	2mg
Carbohydrates:	36g
Sodium:	412mg

*For **3 servings** each serving contains:*

Calories:	179
Fat:	7g
Protein:	5g
Cholesterol:	2mg
Carbohydrates:	24g
Sodium:	275mg

1 medium onion

2 tablespoons extra virgin olive oil

1 tablespoon balsamic vinegar

1 tablespoon white wine

1 tablespoon freshly grated Parmesan cheese

4 slices Italian bread

1. Trim top and bottom of onion. Remove outer skin. Cut halfway through the onion from top to bottom to form an X.

2. Combine the oil, vinegar, wine, and cheese and drizzle over the onion.

3. Place the onion in a ceramic onion baker and microwave for 2 to 4 minutes or until onion is tender. Use on bread or in recipes.

Note: Alternatively, the onion may be baked in an onion baker or an aluminum foil package for 1 hour at 350°F starting in a cold oven.

baked garlic >>

Put away the breath mints, as you can get the phytochemical advantage of this important member of the allium family without the bad breath.

1 whole garlic bulb

1 teaspoon extra virgin olive oil

1. Trim top of the whole garlic bulb so each clove is exposed.

2. Drizzle with olive oil.

3. Place the bulb in a garlic baker and microwave for 1 to 2 minutes until garlic is tender. Use as spread on bread or in recipes.

Note: *Alternatively, the bulb may be baked in a garlic baker or an aluminum foil package for 1 hour at 350°F starting in a cold oven.*

nutrition info

For **2 servings** each serving contains:

Calories:	209
Fat:	4g
Protein:	6g
Cholesterol:	0mg
Carbohydrates:	36g
Sodium:	353mg

For **3 servings** each serving contains:

Calories:	140
Fat:	3g
Protein:	4g
Cholesterol:	0mg
Carbohydrates:	24g
Sodium:	236mg

high performance
fruit butter >>

This nutritious, natural fruit butter can be used by itself as a fruit spread, but it is most amazing as a fat substitute in recipes. We use it in several of ours. Experiment on your own with other dried fruits. Refrigerate any extra in a sealed container.

2 cups water

1 pound pitted prunes

Bring water and prunes to a boil. Simmer for 15 minutes. Drain and puree in a food processor.

simply *salsa* >>

In the United States, salsa has become more popular than catsup. Eat it the old-fashioned but low-fat way, with baked tortilla chips, or as a topping on just about anything.

2 small tomatoes, peeled and diced (see note)

1 hot chili, seeded and diced

⅓ cup diced onion

¼ cup chopped fresh cilantro

1 teaspoon fresh lime juice

1 teaspoon garlic powder

¼ teaspoon salt

Combine all ingredients and allow flavors to develop before using the salsa.

Note: To peel tomatoes, immerse them in boiling water for about 1 minute. Remove carefully. Skins will peel off easily.

nutrition info

*For **2 servings** each serving contains:*

Calories:	44
Fat:	<1g
Protein:	2g
Cholesterol:	0mg
Carbohydrates:	10g
Sodium:	278mg

*For **3 servings** each serving contains:*

Calories:	29
Fat:	<1g
Protein:	1g
Cholesterol:	0mg
Carbohydrates:	7g
Sodium:	185mg

bean relish >>

You can relish this high-fiber dish knowing that it serves up a good dose of protein, too.

*For **2 servings** each serving contains:*

Calories:	394
Fat:	15g
Protein:	17g
Cholesterol:	0mg
Carbohydrates:	51g
Sodium:	3mg

*For **3 servings** each serving contains:*

Calories:	263
Fat:	10g
Protein:	11g
Cholesterol:	0mg
Carbohydrates:	34g
Sodium:	2mg

No-stick cooking spray

1 cup sliced white button mushrooms

½ teaspoon minced fresh chives

¼ teaspoon dried oregano

1 small onion, peeled and thinly sliced

One 15-ounce can kidney beans, drained

2 tablespoons canola oil

Salt and freshly ground black pepper to taste

1. Heat a saucepan over high heat for 30 seconds. Spray with cooking spray and cook the mushrooms, stirring, until softened. Add the chives and oregano. Toss thoroughly and remove from the heat.

2. In a bowl, combine the mushroom mixture with the onion, beans, and oil and toss until ingredients are well mixed. Add salt and pepper. Serve chilled.

confetti relish >>

This relish explodes with color and taste! What an eye- and palate-pleasing way to serve up some vitamin C and beta-carotene.

½ yellow bell pepper, finely diced

½ red bell pepper, finely diced

½ green bell pepper, finely diced

½ cup cider vinegar

3 tablespoons sugar

½ teaspoon mustard seed

½ teaspoon salt

2 drops Tabasco sauce

Combine all ingredients in a microwave-safe dish and microwave on high for 1½ minutes. Chill and serve.

nutrition info

*For **2 servings** each serving contains:*

Calories:	100
Fat:	<1g
Protein:	<1g
Cholesterol:	0mg
Carbohydrates:	26g
Sodium:	535mg

*For **3 servings** each serving contains:*

Calories:	67
Fat:	<1g
Protein:	<1g
Cholesterol:	0mg
Carbohydrates:	17g
Sodium:	357mg

55

dim sum >>

One of our favorite Sunday meals is brunch at an authentic Chinese dim sum restaurant. Creating dim sum at
home removes the aura of the unknown about what you will
be eating, but you also don't have to wait for the little carts
to come around to serve you. Enjoy these four vegetarian
versions of dim sum.

dim sum 1

1½ teaspoons canola oil

1 small onion, peeled and minced

5 white mushrooms, minced

1 scallion, diced

1 teaspoon chopped fresh ginger

¼ cup peas and carrots, frozen

2 tablespoons rice wine

8 thin wonton skins

Soy sauce for dipping

1. In a skillet or wok, heat the oil over medium-
high heat and cook the onion, mushrooms,
scallion, and ginger, stirring, until the onion
and mushrooms are softened, about 5 minutes. Add the peas and carrots and rice wine
and stir until well mixed.

2. Place about 1 to 1½ teaspoons of filling in the
center of each wonton skin. Bring the points
of the wonton skin together and press firmly
to seal the filling inside. Place each wonton in
a vegetable steamer. Continue until all the
skins are filled. Steam for 7 minutes or until
the dough is cooked. Serve with soy sauce.

nutrition info

For **2 servings** each serving
contains:

Calories:	176
Fat:	4g
Protein:	5g
Cholesterol:	3mg
Carbohydrates:	26g
Sodium:	200mg

For **3 servings** each serving
contains:

Calories:	118
Fat:	3g
Protein:	3g
Cholesterol:	2mg
Carbohydrates:	18g
Sodium:	133mg

dim *sum 2*

1½ teaspoons canola oil

1 small onion, peeled and minced

5 white mushrooms, minced

1 scallion, diced

1 teaspoon chopped fresh ginger

1 teaspoon High Performance Fruit Butter (page 52) or prune butter

8 thin wonton skins

Soy sauce for dipping

1. In a skillet or wok, heat the oil over medium-high heat and cook the onion, mushrooms, scallion, and ginger, stirring, until the onion and mushrooms are softened, about 5 minutes. Add the fruit butter and mix until well coated.

2. Place about 1 to 1½ teaspoons of filling in the center of each wonton skin. Bring the points of the wonton skin together and press firmly. Place each wonton in a vegetable steamer. Continue until all the skins are filled. Steam for 7 minutes or until the dough is cooked. Serve with soy sauce.

nutrition info

*For **2 servings** each serving contains:*

Calories:	164
Fat:	4g
Protein:	5g
Cholesterol:	3mg
Carbohydrates:	28g
Sodium:	190mg

*For **3 servings** each serving contains:*

Calories:	109
Fat:	3g
Protein:	3g
Cholesterol:	2mg
Carbohydrates:	18g
Sodium:	127mg

dim *sum 3*

3 ounces low-fat firm tofu

Dash freshly ground black pepper

Dash powdered garlic

Dash Chinese five-spice powder

8 thin wonton skins

Soy sauce for dipping

1. Combine tofu, pepper, garlic, and five-spice powder in a food processor. Process until the tofu and spices are evenly distributed.

2. Place about 1 to 1½ teaspoons of filling in the center of each wonton skin. Bring the points of the wonton skin together and press firmly. Place each wonton in a vegetable steamer. Continue until all the skins are filled. Steam for 7 minutes or until the dough is cooked. Serve with soy sauce.

nutrition info

*For **2 servings** each serving contains:*

Calories:	136
Fat:	2g
Protein:	8g
Cholesterol:	3mg
Carbohydrates:	21g
Sodium:	185mg

*For **3 servings** each serving contains:*

Calories:	91
Fat:	2g
Protein:	5g
Cholesterol:	2mg
Carbohydrates:	14g
Sodium:	124mg

dim *sum 4*

1½ teaspoons canola oil

1 small onion, peeled and minced

5 white mushrooms, minced

2 tablespoons minced yellow bell pepper

3×1-inch slice of turnip, diced

2 tablespoons rice wine

8 thin wonton skins

Soy sauce for dipping

1. In a skillet or wok, heat the oil over medium-high heat and cook the onion, mushrooms, pepper, and turnip, stirring, until the onion and mushrooms are softened, about 5 minutes. Add the rice wine and mix until well coated.

2. Place about 1 to 1½ teaspoons of filling in the center of each wonton skin. Bring the points of the wonton skin together and press firmly. Place each wonton in a vegetable steamer. Continue until all the skins are filled. Steam for 7 minutes or until the dough is cooked. Serve with soy sauce.

nutrition info

*For **2 servings** each serving contains:*

Calories:	176
Fat:	4g
Protein:	5g
Cholesterol:	3mg
Carbohydrates:	27g
Sodium:	205mg

*For **3 servings** each serving contains:*

Calories:	117
Fat:	3g
Protein:	3g
Cholesterol:	2mg
Carbohydrates:	18g
Sodium:	137mg

guacamole >>

You can eat "guac" in a crock. As a dip for your chip, make sure that the chip is a low-fat hit!

*For 2 **servings** each serving contains:*

Calories:	518
Fat:	19g
Protein:	14g
Cholesterol:	0mg
Carbohydrates:	76g
Sodium:	689mg

*For 3 **servings** each serving contains:*

Calories:	345
Fat:	13g
Protein:	9g
Cholesterol:	0mg
Carbohydrates:	51g
Sodium:	460mg

1 cup avocado pieces

2 tablespoons fresh lemon juice

2 tablespoons chopped onion

1 teaspoon minced garlic

2 teaspoons prepared mustard

2 teaspoons fresh dill

6 ounces baked tortilla chips

¼ cup diced tomato

1. Place all the ingredients into a food processor and blend until smooth.

2. Serve chilled with tortilla chips and diced tomatoes.

harissa >>

This is a very spicy Middle Eastern condiment. Make it as spicy as you like by experimenting with the hot chili powder. We use it with our High-Powered Couscous recipe on page 151. Refrigerate any extra in a sealed container.

½ cup vegetable juice

¼ teaspoon ground cumin

¼ teaspoon ground coriander

Hot chili powder to taste

Combine the vegetable juice, cumin, coriander, and chili powder. Mix well and warm in a microwave oven for 20 seconds, or heat in a small pan on medium-low heat for 5 minutes.

nutrition info

For **2 servings** each serving contains:

Calories:	13
Fat:	<1g
Protein:	<1g
Cholesterol:	0mg
Carbohydrates:	3g
Sodium:	221mg

For **3 servings** each serving contains:

Calories:	9
Fat:	<1g
Protein:	<1g
Cholesterol:	0mg
Carbohydrates:	2g
Sodium:	148mg

61

onion
marmalade >>

Four different members of the allium family give the complex flavor to this spread. This marmalade is a favorite on crackers or as a topping on vegetables or starches. The traditional cooking method would take a couple of hours. Therefore, we have reduced the time by using the microwave oven. Times may vary depending on the wattage of your microwave.

1 teaspoon unsalted butter

1 teaspoon extra virgin olive oil

½ pound sliced leeks (white part only)

½ pound yellow onions, peeled and sliced

¼ pound red onions, peeled and sliced

¼ pound shallots, peeled and sliced

Zest of 1 orange

1 tablespoon honey

¾ teaspoon paprika

1. Place the butter, oil, leeks, onions, and shallots in a microwave-safe bowl. Heat on high for 7 to 10 minutes or until the onions are softened and almost melted.

2. Add the orange zest, honey, and paprika and microwave for an additional 5 to 10 minutes.

sushi >>

You don't have to be a trained sushi chef to make these easy
vegetarian appetizers. Wrapped in sea vegetable, these three
maki-style vegetarian sushi are as delicious as they are
impressive.

kappa maki

½ cup cooked short-grain rice

2 teaspoons rice vinegar

1 sheet nori sea vegetable (seaweed)

1 teaspoon toasted sesame seeds (page 112)

¹⁄₁₆ of a cucumber, sliced lengthwise

Pickled ginger and wasabi (optional)

1. Combine the rice and vinegar and mix with a
wooden spoon or paddle. If rice is warm,
allow to cool to room temperature. Place the
nori on a place mat or sushi mat.

2. Crumble the rice over the nori in an even
layer and press down firmly, leaving a 1-inch
space at the top and bottom edges of the nori.

3. Drizzle the sesame seeds in the center of the
rice and place the cucumber on top of the
seeds.

4. Wet your fingers with water and/or water and
rice vinegar and moisten the edges of the
nori. Roll the nori, using the mat as a support.
Roll tightly and lap one moistened end of the
nori over the other. While the mat is wrapped
around the sushi, tap the ends of the roll.

5. Remove the roll from the mat and cut into
8 slices with a dampened knife. Serve with
pickled ginger and wasabi, if desired.

nutrition info

For **2 servings** each serving
contains:

Calories:	81
Fat:	<1g
Protein:	3g
Cholesterol:	0mg
Carbohydrates:	16g
Sodium:	7mg

For **3 servings** each serving
contains:

Calories:	54
Fat:	<1g
Protein:	2g
Cholesterol:	0mg
Carbohydrates:	11g
Sodium:	5mg

k-rae *maki*

½ cup cooked short-grain rice

2 teaspoons rice vinegar

1 sheet nori sea vegetable (seaweed)

1 scallion, sliced lengthwise

2 ounces low-fat firm tofu, sliced into thin strips

Pickled ginger and wasabi (optional)

1. Combine the rice and vinegar and mix with a wooden spoon or paddle. If rice is warm, allow to cool to room temperature. Place the nori on a place mat or sushi mat.

2. Crumble the rice over the nori in an even layer and press down firmly, leaving a 1-inch space at the top and bottom edges of the nori.

3. Place the scallion and tofu down the center of the rice.

4. Wet your fingers with water and/or water and rice vinegar and moisten the edges of the nori. Roll the nori, using the mat as a support. Roll tightly and lap one moistened end of the nori over the other. While the mat is wrapped around the sushi, tap the ends of the roll.

5. Remove the roll from the mat and cut into 8 slices with a dampened knife. Serve with pickled ginger and wasabi, if desired.

ume *maki*

½ cup cooked short-grain rice

2 teaspoons rice vinegar

1 sheet nori sea vegetable (seaweed)

2 tablespoons High Performance Fruit Butter (page 52) or canned prune butter

5 oba leaves or fresh mint (Oba leaves are available at Asian food markets.)

Pickled ginger and wasabi (optional)

1. Combine the rice and vinegar and mix with a wooden spoon or paddle. If rice is warm, allow to cool to room temperature. Place the nori on a place mat or sushi mat.

2. Crumble the rice over the nori in an even layer and press down firmly, leaving a 1-inch space at the top and bottom edges of the nori.

3. Drizzle the High Performance Fruit Butter in the center of the rice and place the oba leaves in a row on top of the fruit butter.

4. Wet your fingers with water and/or water and rice vinegar and moisten the edges of the nori. Roll the nori using the mat as a support. Roll tightly and lap one moistened end of the nori over the other. While the mat is wrapped around the sushi, tap the ends of the roll.

5. Remove the roll from the mat and cut into 8 slices with a dampened knife. Serve with pickled ginger and wasabi, if desired.

nutrition info

For **2 servings** each serving contains:

Calories:	149
Fat:	<1g
Protein:	6g
Cholesterol:	0mg
Carbohydrates:	31g
Sodium:	57mg

For **3 servings** each serving contains:

Calories:	99
Fat:	<1g
Protein:	4g
Cholesterol:	0mg
Carbohydrates:	20g
Sodium:	38mg

super bowl nachos >>

nutrition info

For **2 servings** each serving contains:

Calories:	416
Fat:	9g
Protein:	36g
Cholesterol:	24mg
Carbohydrates:	62g
Sodium:	537mg

For **3 servings** each serving contains:

Calories:	277
Fat:	6g
Protein:	24g
Cholesterol:	16mg
Carbohydrates:	41g
Sodium:	358mg

Usually high in fat, nachos can be low in fat, like these. We make dozens for our annual Super Bowl fest. Super Bowl parties are more than just the game!

Six 6-inch lard-free tortillas (white, whole wheat, or corn)

Garlic salt

Chili powder

8 ounces shredded part-skim cheddar cheese

Chopped green chilies

Cut the tortillas into chip-sized wedges and place on a baking sheet. Sprinkle with seasonings to taste. Toast in 250°F oven for 20 minutes or until golden brown. Remove from the oven and top each wedge with shredded cheese and chilies to taste. Return to the oven for 5 minutes or until the cheese melts.

world cup
veggie dip >>

More great party food for people who believe that football should not be played with the hands!

½ cup plain, nonfat yogurt

½ teaspoon low-fat mayonnaise

1 tablespoon chopped onion

½ teaspoon finely chopped sweet red pepper

½ teaspoon finely chopped sweet green pepper

½ teaspoon peeled and finely chopped
  cucumber

¼ teaspoon dill weed

⅛ teaspoon garlic powder

Mix all the ingredients together and chill in the refrigerator for 2 hours before serving. Serve with vegetable strips and low-fat chips.

nutrition info

*For **2 servings** each serving contains:*

Calories:	40
Fat:	<1g
Protein:	4g
Cholesterol:	1mg
Carbohydrates:	6g
Sodium:	54mg

*For **3 servings** each serving contains:*

Calories:	27
Fat:	<1g
Protein:	2g
Cholesterol:	<1mg
Carbohydrates:	4g
Sodium:	36mg

yogurt cheese >>

YIELD: SIXTEEN **1**-TABLESPOON SERVINGS

This recipe, created for The High Performance Cookbook, *is included as a substitute for nonfat cream cheese, which is loaded with chemical additives. We use it in other recipes throughout this book, but it can also be enjoyed plain on a bagel or spiced up with herbs or fruit.*

nutrition info

for **16 servings (1 table-spoon each)** *each serving contains:*

Calories:	7.5
Fat:	0g
Protein:	<1g
Cholesterol:	<1mg
Carbohydrates:	1g
Sodium:	11mg

8 ounces plain nonfat yogurt

Cheesecloth or a yogurt cheese sieve

1. Pour the yogurt into the cheesecloth or sieve and place over a clean jar so that the liquid drains from the solid without the solid touching the liquid. If using a cheesecloth, secure it to the jar with a rubber band. Refrigerate while draining. The longer you drain the yogurt, the firmer the cheese product. (We recommend draining overnight.)

2. Discard or save the liquid whey. It is high in riboflavin and can be added to a soup or juice.

3. The yogurt cheese will remain fresh for up to 2 weeks if stored in a sealed container in the refrigerator. Other ingredients, such as herbs or fruit, can be added to the cheese to make unique flavors, though this can shorten the shelf life.

>>>

sumptuous
soups

very vegetable
soup >>

This variation on an American classic is a mainstay of a vegetarian diet. It is an excellent source of phytochemicals.

1 tablespoon corn oil

1 medium onion, peeled and chopped

1 garlic clove, peeled and minced

1 medium parsnip, scraped and chopped

1 medium carrot, chopped

1 celery stalk, chopped

2 plum tomatoes, chopped

1 cup frozen corn kernels, thawed

3 cups vegetable stock (page 71)

2 tablespoons minced fresh parsley

1 teaspoon minced fresh cilantro

⅛ teaspoon freshly ground black pepper

Salt or low-sodium soy sauce to taste

1. In a nonstick saucepan over medium heat, heat the oil and cook the onion and garlic, stirring, until softened, about 3 minutes. Add the parsnip, carrot, and celery, and cook, stirring occasionally, until vegetables are tender, 12 to 15 minutes. Add the tomatoes and corn and cook another 5 minutes.

2. Add the stock, raise the heat, and bring to a boil. Reduce heat to low, add 1 tablespoon parsley and the cilantro and pepper, and simmer for 20 minutes, or until vegetables are soft. Before serving, add remaining parsley and salt or soy sauce to taste.

basic vegetable stock I

You know the expression, "Don't throw the baby out with the bath water." Well, don't throw the nutrients out with the cooking water. This recipe conserves many of the water-soluble nutrients lost in cooking water. This is a classic vegetarian type of stock and will be used in many recipes. (Read discussion on vegetable stock in Chapter 2, page 37.)

Cooking water from vegetables, except those from the cabbage family (e.g., cabbage, cauliflower, Brussels sprouts, broccoli)

Salt or low-sodium soy sauce to taste (optional)

1. Collect the cooking water from all vegetables and mix together. Store in a tightly closed jar in the refrigerator. This stock should stay fresh for about 7 days.

2. Before using, heat the stock and add salt or soy sauce to taste, if desired.

basic vegetable stock II

If you don't save your vegetable water, this method works to give you a quick, easy, flavorful broth. Onions and garlic are from the allium family of vegetables, giving a very tasty broth, and also are a rich source of phytochemicals.

1 medium onion, peeled and diced

2 garlic cloves, peeled and minced

3 tablespoons low-sodium soy sauce

6 cups water

Place the onion and garlic in a nonstick pan over medium-low heat and cook until soft, about 4 minutes. Add soy sauce and water and bring to a boil. The stock can be used immediately or stored in the refrigerator in a tightly closed jar for up to 7 days.

nutrition info

For **2 servings** each serving contains:

Calories:	47
Fat:	<1g
Protein:	3g
Cholesterol:	0mg
Carbohydrates:	9g
Sodium:	782mg

For **3 servings** each serving contains:

Calories:	32
Fat:	<1g
Protein:	2g
Cholesterol:	0mg
Carbohydrates:	6g
Sodium:	521mg

71

black bean soup >>

This traditional Southwestern soup, an excellent source of fiber, will have you shouting "Howdy."

1 medium onion, peeled and sliced

1 celery stalk, chopped

1 tablespoon safflower oil

One 15-ounce can black beans with liquid

¼ teaspoon salt

⅛ teaspoon dried basil

¼ teaspoon celery seed

1 small bay leaf

1 teaspoon fresh lemon juice

Tamari sauce or soy sauce to taste

Sprigs of fresh parsley (optional)

1 hard-boiled egg, peeled and sliced (optional)

1. In a saucepan over high heat, cook the onion and celery in the oil until tender, about 3 minutes. Add the beans, salt, basil, celery seed, and bay leaf. Cover and simmer for 15 minutes.

2. Remove the bay leaf and put the bean mixture in a blender. Add the lemon juice and tamari and blend until smooth. Garnish with parsley and egg slices before serving, if desired.

carrot soup >>

After eating this soup rich in beta-carotene, you will feel so great you won't have to say, "What's up, Doc?"

1 medium onion, peeled and diced

1 tablespoon butter

1 pound carrots, scraped and sliced

2 cups vegetable broth (page 71)

One 12-ounce can evaporated skim milk

Salt and freshly ground black pepper to taste

1. In a 2-quart saucepan over low heat, cook the onion in the butter until softened, about 5 minutes.

2. Add the carrots and broth to the pot. Raise the heat to high and bring to a boil. Reduce the heat to low and simmer until the carrots are tender, about 10 minutes. Add the evaporated milk and simmer for 3 minutes or until soup returns to a low boil. Add the salt and pepper.

3. Remove from the heat, puree in a food processor or blender, and serve.

nutrition info

For 2 servings each serving contains:

Calories:	328
Fat:	8g
Protein:	16g
Cholesterol:	22mg
Carbohydrates:	50g
Sodium:	994mg

For 3 servings each serving contains:

Calories:	219
Fat:	5g
Protein:	11g
Cholesterol:	14mg
Carbohydrates:	33g
Sodium:	662mg

sunset soup >>

The marriage of beets and orange juice makes a beautiful picture resembling a sunset. This soup proves that oranges aren't just for breakfast. Nutritionally, this soup is an excellent source of vitamin C.

1 medium beet, peeled and diced (about 1¼ cups)

1½ cups water

⅛ teaspoon salt

⅛ teaspoon ground nutmeg

1 cup canned tomato puree

4 ounces frozen orange juice concentrate

Mint leaves

1. In a covered saucepan over medium heat, boil the beets in the water with the salt and nutmeg until the beets are tender, about 15 minutes. Remove from heat and chill thoroughly.

2. Just before serving, stir the tomato puree and orange juice into the beet mixture. Serve in chilled bowls garnished with mint leaves.

corn chowder >>

A robust soup that has warmed the cockles of many a New England sailor's heart. But what exactly is a cockle?

2 tablespoons corn oil

1 small onion, peeled and diced

8 ounces frozen corn kernels

1 parsnip, scraped and diced

1 tablespoon brown sugar

⅛ teaspoon salt

⅛ teaspoon freshly ground black pepper

½ cup vegetable broth (page 71)

½ cup skim milk

1 cup water

1 tablespoon cornstarch, dissolved in 2 tablespoons cold water

1. Heat the oil in a skillet over medium heat. Add the onion and cook until tender, about 3 minutes.

2. Add the corn and parsnip. Reduce heat to low and cook, stirring, for 5 minutes.

3. Add the sugar, salt, and pepper. Then add the broth, milk, water, and dissolved cornstarch to soup. Mix thoroughly and simmer for 10 minutes. Serve immediately.

nutrition info

*For **2 servings** each serving contains:*

Calories:	269
Fat:	7g
Protein:	7g
Cholesterol:	1mg
Carbohydrates:	49g
Sodium:	333mg

*For **3 servings** each serving contains:*

Calories:	180
Fat:	5g
Protein:	4g
Cholesterol:	<1mg
Carbohydrates:	32g
Sodium:	222mg

miso soup >>

Miso is a fermented soy bean paste and a staple of Japanese cuisine. It is an excellent source of phytoestrogens, which may help to reduce the risk of hormone-related cancer, such as breast and prostate cancer. We prefer mild shiro *miso.*

nutrition info

For **2 servings** each serving contains:

Calories:	176
Fat:	7g
Protein:	11g
Cholesterol:	0mg
Carbohydrates:	19g
Sodium:	1294mg

For **3 servings** each serving contains:

Calories:	118
Fat:	5g
Protein:	7g
Cholesterol:	0mg
Carbohydrates:	13g
Sodium:	863mg

1 carrot, peeled and chopped

1 small onion, peeled and sliced

½ tablespoon corn oil

3 cups water

1½ teaspoons shredded wakami sea vegetable (seaweed)

¼ cup miso

4 ounces firm tofu, cubed

1. In a nonstick pan over medium-high heat, cook the carrot and onion in the oil, stirring, until softened, about 5 minutes. Add the water and wakami, reduce the heat to low, and simmer for 10 minutes to blend flavors. Remove from heat.

2. Remove ¼ cup of the broth to a small bowl and cool for 1 to 2 minutes. Mix the cooled broth with the miso to make a thin paste. Add the miso paste to the broth mixture and stir well. Add the tofu and serve.

mushroom barley
soup >>

Barley is a hearty grain closely associated with the making of beer. But for those cold winter nights when soup keeps you warm, avoid the six-pack and instead make this source of resorylic acid and lignins.

¼ cup pearl barley

3¼ cups vegetable broth (page 71)

1 tablespoon soy sauce

2 tablespoons dry sherry

1 fresh garlic clove, peeled and minced

½ cup chopped onion

½ medium parsnip, scraped and sliced

½ medium carrot, sliced

1 tablespoon unsalted butter

8 ounces mushrooms, sliced

¼ teaspoon freshly ground black pepper

nutrition info

For **2 servings** each serving contains:

Calories:	273
Fat:	8g
Protein:	7g
Cholesterol:	16mg
Carbohydrates:	42g
Sodium:	1399mg

For **3 servings** each serving contains:

Calories:	182
Fat:	6g
Protein:	5g
Cholesterol:	10mg
Carbohydrates:	28g
Sodium:	932mg

1. In a stock pot over low heat, cover and cook the barley in ¾ cup broth until tender, about 20 minutes. Do not let the broth boil away. Add the remaining broth, soy sauce, and sherry, and continue to cook.

2. Meanwhile, in a skillet over medium heat, cook the garlic, onion, parsnip, and carrot in the butter until softened, about 15 minutes. Add the mushrooms and cook another 5 minutes, or until the vegetables are tender. Add the vegetable mixture and remaining pan juices to the simmering barley.

3. Sprinkle with the pepper and cook, covered, over low heat about 30 minutes.

pocahontas
soup >>

A version of a staple food of Pocahontas and the American settlers, John Smith's favorite soup is rich in beta-carotene.

1 medium onion, peeled and chopped

1 tablespoon unsalted butter

¼ teaspoon curry powder

1¼ cups vegetable broth (page 71)

1 cup mashed pumpkin (fresh or canned)

1 cup evaporated skim milk

¾ teaspoon salt

1 teaspoon fresh chopped parsley or
  ⅓ teaspoon dried parsley

1 teaspoon ground nutmeg

4 tablespoons Yogurt Cheese (page 68)
  or nonfat sour cream

2 teaspoons chopped fresh chives

1. In a nonstick saucepan over medium heat, cook the onion in the butter, stirring, until softened, about 3 minutes. Sprinkle with curry powder and cook 1 more minute. Put the mixture in a blender with ½ cup broth. Blend 30 seconds and return to saucepan. Add the remaining broth, pumpkin, milk, salt, and chervil. Heat thoroughly, but do not boil.

2. When ready to serve, add the nutmeg, a dollop of Yogurt Cheese or sour cream, and a sprinkling of chopped chives to bowl.

spinach borscht >>

A traditional Russian favorite based originally on beets,
this version is one that even Popeye could love!

1 pound fresh spinach, washed well

3 cups boiling water

⅛ cup fresh lemon juice

Salt to taste

¼ cucumber, diced

2 radishes, thinly sliced

1 scallion (white and green parts), diced

½ cup Yogurt Cheese (page 68) or nonfat sour
cream

1. Cut the spinach into 1-inch pieces. Add
spinach to the boiling water and cook over
medium-high heat for 10 minutes.

2. Add the lemon juice and salt. Continue cooking for an additional 10 minutes. Remove
from the heat.

3. Chill the soup. Add the cucumber, radishes,
and scallion. Serve with 1 heaping teaspoon
of Yogurt Cheese per 1-cup serving, or 1 level
teaspoon per 5-ounce serving size.

nutrition info

For **2 servings** each serving
contains:

Calories:	104
Fat:	<1g
Protein:	10g
Cholesterol:	2mg
Carbohydrates:	18g
Sodium:	326mg

For **3 servings** each serving
contains:

Calories:	70
Fat:	<1g
Protein:	7g
Cholesterol:	1mg
Carbohydrates:	12g
Sodium:	217mg

best of autumn soup >>

This soup combines the incredible taste sensation of fresh apples and squash.

1 small butternut squash

1 medium leek

2 teaspoons canola oil

1 medium Granny Smith apple, cored and diced

⅛ teaspoon dried thyme

1⅔ cups vegetable broth (page 71)

1 bay leaf, whole and intact

Dash ground ginger

Dash ground cinnamon

½ teaspoon pure maple syrup

¾ teaspoon honey

1 teaspoon fresh lemon juice

Freshly ground black pepper to taste

2 tablespoons evaporated skim milk

1. Microwave the whole squash for 10 minutes on high until tender. Cut open, scoop out the seeds, and chop. Set aside.

2. Remove the dark leaves on the leek. Wash the leek thoroughly. Dice the light green leaves and white portion.

3. In a 2-quart saucepan over low heat, heat the canola oil. Cook the leek and apple in the oil until softened, 3 to 5 minutes. Add the thyme.

4. Add the squash, vegetable broth, bay leaf, ginger, cinnamon, maple syrup, honey, and lemon juice. Raise the heat to high and bring soup to a boil. Reduce the heat to low and cook for 30 minutes. Add the black pepper.

5. Remove the bay leaf. Add the milk. Puree in a food processor until smooth and serve.

tarato >>

This yogurt soup, native to Bulgaria, is very refreshing after a swim on a hot day. Eating active yogurt culture has been linked to good health and longevity in many parts of the world.

2 cups plain, nonfat yogurt

½ cup water

1 cucumber, diced and peeled

1 tablespoon extra virgin olive oil

1 teaspoon vinegar

Salt to taste

¼ cup slivered almonds

Combine the yogurt, water, cucumber, olive oil, and vinegar. Mix thoroughly and add salt. Add the almonds and refrigerate for 2 to 3 hours or overnight to allow flavors to blend. Serve chilled.

nutrition info

*For **2 servings** each serving contains:*

Calories:	236
Fat:	8g
Protein:	17g
Cholesterol:	4mg
Carbohydrates:	25g
Sodium:	234mg

*For **3 servings** each serving contains:*

Calories:	157
Fat:	6g
Protein:	11g
Cholesterol:	3mg
Carbohydrates:	17g
Sodium:	156mg

three bean soup >>

Our Three Bean Soup actually contains two beans and a variety of peas.

1 cup water

½ cup dried lentils

1 tablespoon canola oil

1 small onion, peeled and chopped

¼ cup chopped green bell pepper

1 cup frozen black-eyed peas

1 cup frozen speckled butter beans

1 cup vegetable broth (page 71)

6 sun-dried tomatoes, sliced and rehydrated in hot water for 5 minutes

1 cup (8 ounces) tomato juice (preferably V8 brand)

¼ cup red wine

1 teaspoon fresh lemon juice

1. In a large saucepan, bring the water to a boil over medium-high heat and cook the lentils for 30 minutes. Drain and set aside.

2. Heat the oil in a saucepan over medium heat. Add the onion and cook, stirring, until softened, about 5 minutes. Add the green pepper and cook an additional 5 minutes.

3. Add the lentils, black-eyed peas, and butter beans to the saucepan. Add the vegetable broth, tomatoes, and tomato juice. Reduce the heat to low and cook for 10 minutes. Add the wine and cook for 5 minutes.

4. Add the lemon juice and serve.

riskless bisque >>

This vegetable bisque takes the risk out of the classic high-fat bisque and combines eggplant and zucchini in a unique blend of flavors. It is also an excellent electrolyte replacer.

1 small onion, peeled and chopped

1 teaspoon unsalted butter

2 large carrots, scraped and chopped

2 large celery stalks, trimmed and chopped

1 small zucchini, chopped

1 small eggplant, chopped

¾ cup water

½ teaspoon salt

⅛ teaspoon white pepper

12 ounces evaporated skim milk

1 tablespoon cornstarch, dissolved in 2 tablespoons cold water

2 sprigs fresh parsley, chopped

1. In a large saucepan over low heat, cook the onion in butter, stirring, until softened, about 5 minutes.

2. Add the remaining vegetables and mix thoroughly. Cook, stirring, for 5 more minutes. Add the water, cover the pan, and cook for 5 minutes.

3. Add the salt, pepper, and milk to the vegetables. Cook for 10 minutes. Add the dissolved cornstarch, stirring until thickened.

4. Garnish with the parsley and serve.

nutrition info

*For **2 servings** each serving contains:*

Calories:	307
Fat:	3g
Protein:	18g
Cholesterol:	11mg
Carbohydrates:	56g
Sodium:	825mg

*For **3 servings** each serving contains:*

Calories:	205
Fat:	2g
Protein:	12g
Cholesterol:	8mg
Carbohydrates:	37g
Sodium:	550mg

CHAPTER FIVE >>>

bread
bonanza

breakfast bars
extraordinaire >>

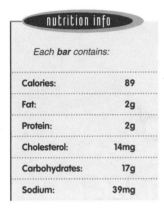

nutrition info

*Each **bar** contains:*

Calories:	89
Fat:	2g
Protein:	2g
Cholesterol:	14mg
Carbohydrates:	17g
Sodium:	39mg

YIELD: **18** BARS

These crispy bars are a desirable substitute for the higher-fat granola bars or rubbery, nonfat breakfast bars on the market. Have three bars with a glass of orange juice and skim milk and you'll be energized for a rigorous morning. Store the bars for up to one week in an airtight container.

2 tablespoons sweet butter, softened

2 tablespoons applesauce

½ cup sugar

1 large egg

¾ cup unbleached all-purpose flour

¾ cup whole-wheat flour

⅛ teaspoon baking powder

¾ cup Grape Nuts brand cereal

1. Preheat the oven to 400°F.

2. Blend all of the ingredients with 2 table-spoons of the Grape Nuts cereal in a bowl. Roll the dough into bars about 2 inches long and ½ inch in diameter. Spread the remaining cereal on a plate and roll the bars into the extra cereal to coat. Place the bars on a non-stick cookie sheet and bake for 15 minutes or until slightly browned. Cool completely before storing to maintain crispness.

chocolate raspberry muffins >>

YIELD: **12** MUFFINS

This healthful choice for the chocoholic can be made even lower in fat by substituting fat-free yogurt.

No-stick cooking spray

2 ounces unsweetened chocolate, melted

8 ounces low-fat raspberry yogurt

1 teaspoon vanilla extract

1 cup unbleached all-purpose flour

½ cup sugar

1 teaspoon baking powder

⅛ teaspoon salt

2 egg whites, beaten to soft peaks

1. Preheat the oven to 350°F. Spray a muffin tin with cooking spray and set aside.

2. In a bowl, combine the chocolate, yogurt, and vanilla. Set aside. In a separate bowl, combine the flour, sugar, baking powder, and salt. Mix the dry ingredients into the chocolate mixture until well blended. Fold in the egg whites.

3. Fill muffin tins about ¾ full with batter and bake for 15 minutes or until well done.

Note: Add ⅓ cup dried raspberries if desired.

nutrition info

Each **muffin** contains:

Calories:	119
Fat:	3g
Protein:	2g
Cholesterol:	1mg
Carbohydrates:	22g
Sodium:	82mg

corn bread muffins >>

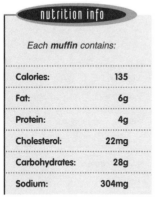

nutrition info

*Each **muffin** contains:*

Calories:	135
Fat:	6g
Protein:	4g
Cholesterol:	22mg
Carbohydrates:	28g
Sodium:	304mg

YIELD: **10** MUFFINS

Hot corn bread is a treasured Southern delicacy. This low-fat version is aimed at high-performance living. This recipe can also be made in an 8-inch square pan. You'll be whistling Dixie before you know it!

No-stick cooking spray

1 large egg

1 cup buttermilk

¼ cup honey

3 tablespoons unsweetened applesauce

1 cup coarse yellow cornmeal

1 cup unbleached all-purpose flour

2 teaspoons baking powder

½ teaspoon baking soda

½ teaspoon salt

1. Preheat the oven to 425°F. Spray a muffin tin with cooking spray.

2. In a bowl, beat together the egg, buttermilk, and honey. Add the applesauce and beat again. In a separate bowl, combine the dry ingredients. Add the dry ingredients to the liquid ingredients and mix until all the ingredients are blended. Do not overmix. Fill muffin tins about ¾ full with batter.

3. Bake for 20 minutes.

cranana bread >>

*The cranberries add a zingy zest to classic banana bread.
You can eat this like cake!*

No-stick cooking spray

1¾ cups all-purpose flour

1½ teaspoons baking powder

¼ teaspoon salt

⅛ teaspoon baking soda

¼ cup canola oil

½ cup sugar

3 egg whites

1 medium banana, peeled and mashed

½ cup dried cranberries

1. Preheat the oven to 325°F. Spray a loaf pan with cooking spray and set aside.

2. In a large bowl, combine all the ingredients and mix well. Pour the batter into the loaf pan.

3. Bake for 1 hour.

nutrition info

*For **8 slices** each slice contains:*

Calories:	231
Fat:	7g
Protein:	4g
Cholesterol:	0mg
Carbohydrates:	38g
Sodium:	199mg

*For **10 slices** each slice contains:*

Calories:	185
Fat:	6g
Protein:	3g
Cholesterol:	0mg
Carbohydrates:	30g
Sodium:	159mg

focaccia >>

While this bread is not for the automatic bread machine, it is for the amateur bread maker. Although somewhat time consuming, this bread is well worth the effort. A staple food of northern Italy, focaccia is commonly drizzled with olive oil, covered with baked garlic, and topped with grilled vegetables.

nutrition info

For **8 slices** each slice contains:

Calories:	227
Fat:	4g
Protein:	6g
Cholesterol:	0mg
Carbohydrates:	41g
Sodium:	402mg

For **10 slices** each slice contains:

Calories:	182
Fat:	3g
Protein:	4g
Cholesterol:	0mg
Carbohydrates:	33g
Sodium:	322mg

1 package active dry yeast

1¼ cups water

2 teaspoons honey

3 cups unbleached all-purpose flour

2 tablespoons extra virgin olive oil

1½ teaspoons coarse salt

¼ cup semolina flour

Freshly ground black pepper

1. In a bowl, beat the yeast, water, and honey and 2 cups of the flour together. Let the mixture stand overnight, for 10 to 24 hours, at room temperature.

2. Add the oil, ½ teaspoon salt, and the remaining flour to make a soft dough. Knead for 10 minutes and then let rise for 1 hour.

3. Divide the dough in half and dust each with the semolina flour. Place the dough on an oiled baking sheet. Let the dough rise for 30 minutes.

4. Push down the dough and allow it to rise for 30 to 40 minutes.

5. Preheat the oven to 425°F. Sprinkle the dough with remaining salt and pepper. Push down the dough and allow it to rise again for 30 to 40 minutes.

6. Place a pan of water on the lowest shelf of the oven. Bake the bread at 425°F on the middle shelf of the oven for 12 minutes. Serve warm or at room temperature.

mighty muffins >>

YIELD: **12** MUFFINS

Tell your kids these are "Mighty Morphin" muffins, and they'll eat them up. These great low-fat muffins are easy to make and turn out great every time. Make them part of your everyday high-carbohydrate diet, and remember to pack them along for extra energy on the trail. Freeze them for long-term freshness.

nutrition info

Each **muffin** contains:

Calories:	125
Fat:	2g
Protein:	3g
Cholesterol:	20mg
Carbohydrates:	23g
Sodium:	267mg

1 large egg

1 cup buttermilk

¼ cup honey

1 cup coarse yellow cornmeal

1 cup unbleached all-purpose flour

2 teaspoons baking powder

½ teaspoon baking soda

½ teaspoon salt

1½ tablespoons sweet butter, melted

3 tablespoons dried sweetened cranberries

No-stick cooking spray

1. Preheat the oven to 425°F.

2. In a large bowl, beat the egg, buttermilk, honey, and applesauce. In another bowl, combine the cornmeal, flour, baking powder, baking soda, and salt. Add the dry ingredients to the egg mixture, stir in the melted butter and cranberries, and blend well. Spray a muffin tin with no-stick cooking spray. Drop the batter into the muffin tins, filling each halfway.

3. Bake for 20 minutes.

orange cinnamon bobke >>

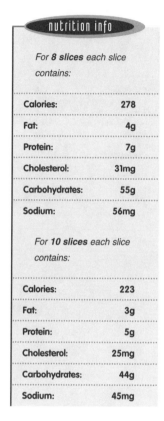

For **8 slices** each slice contains:

Calories:	278
Fat:	4g
Protein:	7g
Cholesterol:	31mg
Carbohydrates:	55g
Sodium:	56mg

For **10 slices** each slice contains:

Calories:	223
Fat:	3g
Protein:	5g
Cholesterol:	25mg
Carbohydrates:	44g
Sodium:	45mg

This recipe has been designed for a bread machine. Indigenous to Eastern Europe and made famous on television, bobke is positioned to be the trendy bread of the twenty-first century. The orange zest in this recipe is a concentrated source of monoterpenes, a strong anticancer agent.

¼ cup honey

½ cup skim milk

2 tablespoons sweet butter

1 extra-large egg

1 egg white

2 teaspoons grated orange zest

2¾ cups unbleached all-purpose flour

2 teaspoons ground cinnamon

1 package active dry yeast

½ cup raisins

¼ cup brown sugar

1. Place all the wet ingredients into the bottom of the bread machine pan.

2. Add the orange zest, flour, and 1 teaspoon cinnamon. Sprinkle the yeast over the dry ingredients and place the pan into the bread machine.

3. Set the machine to the raisin bread cycle with 2 kneads. Add the raisins almost at the end of the second knead cycle. At the end of the second knead cycle, sprinkle the brown sugar and remaining teaspoon of cinnamon on top of the dough. Bake according to the machine's instructions.

peanut butter and jelly bread >>

This recipe has been designed for a bread machine. For the adult with the inner child craving PB&Js, this healthful bread will take you back to those memories of idyllic childhood.

1 cup water

½ cup peanut butter

3 cups unbleached all-purpose flour

¼ cup sugar

½ teaspoon salt

1 package active dry yeast

½ cup dried strawberries or other dried fruit

1. Place the water and peanut butter into the bottom of the bread machine pan.

2. Add the flour, sugar, and salt. Sprinkle the yeast over the dry ingredients and place the pan into the bread machine.

3. Set the machine to the raisin bread cycle with 2 knead cycles. Add the dried fruit almost at the end of the second knead cycle. Bake according to the machine's instructions.

nutrition info

For **8 slices** each slice contains:

Calories:	340
Fat:	9g
Protein:	9g
Cholesterol:	0mg
Carbohydrates:	57g
Sodium:	212mg

For **10 slices** each slice contains:

Calories:	272
Fat:	7g
Protein:	7g
Cholesterol:	0mg
Carbohydrates:	46g
Sodium:	170mg

93

pumpernickel bread >>

This recipe has been designed for a bread machine. Our daughters call it "chocolate bread," and they are absolutely right! This multigrain bread gets its color from cocoa and its unique flavor from coffee, cocoa, and raisins.

1 cup water

½ cup brewed coffee

¼ cup molasses

2 tablespoons canola oil

⅓ cup cocoa powder

1 cup rye flour

1 cup whole-wheat flour

1½ cups unbleached all-purpose flour

¼ cup brown sugar

2 teaspoons salt

2 packages active dry yeast

½ cup raisins

1. Place the water, coffee, molasses, and oil into the bottom of the bread machine pan.

2. Add the cocoa powder, flours, brown sugar, and salt. Sprinkle the yeast over the dry ingredients and place the pan into the bread machine.

3. Set the machine so that it kneads the dough 3 times. This may need to be done manually.

4. Add the raisins shortly before the end of the third knead cycle. Bake according to the machine's instructions for whole-wheat breads.

pumpkin scones >>

YIELD: **12** SCONES

Great Britain may have given us the scone, but the Colonists added the pumpkin for this nutrient-dense treat.

1 cup whole-wheat flour

1 teaspoon baking powder

¼ teaspoon salt

¼ teaspoon ground cinnamon

¼ teaspoon ground nutmeg

¾ cup honey

1 cup pumpkin, fresh cooked or canned

1 large egg, lightly beaten

1 teaspoon vanilla

½ cup raisins, chopped walnuts, or chocolate chips (optional)

1. Preheat the oven to 350°F. Grease a cookie sheet.

2. In a bowl, combine the flour, baking powder, salt, cinnamon, and nutmeg. Set aside. In another large bowl, combine the honey, pumpkin, egg, and vanilla and mix until blended.

3. Stir the dry ingredients into the wet ingredients and mix until blended. Add raisins, walnuts, or chocolate chips, if using.

4. Drop 2 tablespoons of batter for each scone on the cookie sheet and repeat until the batter is used up. Bake for 10 to 15 minutes or until the scones spring back when pressed lightly.

nutrition info

*For **4 servings of 3 scones**, each serving contains:*

Calories:	330
Fat:	2g
Protein:	6g
Cholesterol:	53mg
Carbohydrates:	78g
Sodium:	276mg

*For **6 servings of 2 scones**, each serving contains:*

Calories:	220
Fat:	1g
Protein:	4g
Cholesterol:	35mg
Carbohydrates:	52g
Sodium:	184mg

rye bread >>

This recipe has been designed for a bread machine. This fragrant bread is the perfect accompaniment to Mushroom Barley Soup (page 77). Caraway seeds are a source of monoterpenes, a strong anticancer agent.

1 cup water

2 tablespoons canola oil

2 tablespoons sugar

1 teaspoon salt

2 teaspoons caraway seeds

2¼ cups bread flour

½ cup rye flour

1 package active dry yeast

1. Place the water and oil into the bottom of your bread machine pan.

2. Add all the remaining ingredients except for the yeast. Sprinkle the yeast over the dry ingredients and place the pan into your bread machine.

3. Set the machine to a regular whole-grain cycle with 2 kneads. Bake according to the machine's instructions.

nutrition info

For **8 slices** each slice contains:

Calories:	181
Fat:	4g
Protein:	5g
Cholesterol:	0mg
Carbohydrates:	31g
Sodium:	268mg

For **10 slices** each slice contains:

Calories:	144
Fat:	3g
Protein:	4g
Cholesterol:	0mg
Carbohydrates:	25g
Sodium:	215mg

beer bread >>

This bread is for those who believe the three staples of the American diet are flour, sugar, and beer. Note that the beer provides the leavening and taste; the alcohol cooks off.

No-stick cooking spray

One 12-ounce can beer

3 cups all-purpose flour

⅓ cup sugar

1. Spray a loaf pan with cooking spray. In a large bowl, mix the beer, flour, and sugar together and pour it into the pan.

2. Bake in a non-preheated oven at 350°F for 1 hour.

nutrition info

*For **8 slices** each slice contains:*

Calories:	221
Fat:	<1g
Protein:	5g
Cholesterol:	0mg
Carbohydrates:	46g
Sodium:	3mg

*For **10 slices** each slice contains:*

Calories:	177
Fat:	<1g
Protein:	4g
Cholesterol:	0mg
Carbohydrates:	37g
Sodium:	3mg

97

*romantic rice
and
gorgeous
grains*

caribbean wild rice >>

This rice dish is truly wild with the taste of nuts and bananas. It is packed with copper, iron, magnesium, potassium, selenium, folacin, and most of the B vitamins.

2¾ cups water

1 cup wild rice

1 ripe banana, sliced into disks

¼ cup pecans

1. Bring the water to a boil over high heat in a saucepan. Add the rice, banana, and pecans.

2. Cover the saucepan and reduce the heat to low. Cook for 1 hour or until the water is absorbed and the rice is tender.

barley pilaf >>

Aside from mushroom barley soup, barley is not a common ingredient in American cooking. But nutrition scientists tell us that the water-soluble fibers in barley will do as much for our arteries as oatmeal. So enjoy this easy way to add more barley, and great carbs, to your diet.

⅓ cup pearl barley

4 ounces fresh mushrooms, sliced

½ medium onion, peeled and chopped

¼ teaspoon salt

½ teaspoon safflower oil

No-stick cooking spray

½ cup frozen peas, thawed

2 cups vegetable broth (page 71)

¼ cup toasted sliced almonds

2 tablespoons chopped fresh parsley

1. Preheat the oven to 350°F.

2. In a nonstick skillet over medium heat, cook the barley, mushrooms, onion, and salt in the oil, stirring, until the vegetables are soft, about 5 minutes. Lightly coat a 1-quart casserole with the cooking spray and add the barley mixture, peas, and vegetable broth.

3. Bake uncovered for 50 minutes. Stir in the almonds and parsley and serve.

nutrition info

For **2 servings** each serving contains:

Calories:	315
Fat:	12g
Protein:	10g
Cholesterol:	0mg
Carbohydrates:	45g
Sodium:	911mg

For **3 servings** each serving contains:

Calories:	211
Fat:	8g
Protein:	7g
Cholesterol:	0mg
Carbohydrates:	30g
Sodium:	608mg

broccoli risotto >>

Just north of Cortena, Italy, there are Alpine meadows of gold and green that are the inspiration for this high-antioxidant dish. So if you've climbed in the Alps, this dish will fuel your body and your memories.

nutrition info

For **2 servings** *each serving contains:*

Calories:	458
Fat:	16g
Protein:	11g
Cholesterol:	5mg
Carbohydrates:	67g
Sodium:	384mg

For **3 servings** *each serving contains:*

Calories:	305
Fat:	11g
Protein:	7g
Cholesterol:	3mg
Carbohydrates:	44g
Sodium:	256mg

2 tablespoons extra virgin olive oil

1 small onion, peeled and chopped

1 garlic clove, peeled and minced

2 teaspoons chopped fresh parsley

½ cup chopped broccoli florets

1 cup Arborio rice or short-grain rice

3 cups low-sodium vegetable broth (page 71)

2 tablespoons freshly grated Parmesan cheese

1. In a large skillet, heat 1 tablespoon oil over medium heat for 1 minute. Add the onion and garlic and cook, stirring, until softened, about 5 minutes.

2. Add the parsley and broccoli. Cook, stirring, for 5 minutes more.

3. Add the rice and ½ cup broth, stirring to prevent sticking. Add the remaining broth, ½ cup at a time. Wait until the broth is absorbed before adding more broth. Continue to stir as needed.

4. Add the remaining tablespoon oil and the Parmesan cheese. Toss to mix and cook 2 minutes more.

the best granola
you've ever had >>

Honestly, you'll like this granola better than the high-fat, commercial versions. Eat it dry for a great snack or with skim milk to boost the protein and calcium content. This stores well in an airtight container in a cool place for several weeks.

1 cup rolled oats

½ cup Kashi ready-to-eat cereal

⅛ cup honey

1 tablespoon canola oil

1 tablespoon water

¼ cup dried, sweetened cranberries

¼ cup golden raisins

2 tablespoons plus 2 teaspoons slivered almonds

1. Preheat the oven to 300°F.

2. In a large bowl, mix together the oats, Kashi, and honey. In a separate bowl, combine the oil and water and pour over the oat mixture. Blend well.

3. Spread the mixture evenly on a nonstick cookie sheet and bake for 10 minutes. Stir and return to oven for another 10 minutes. Remove from the oven and add the cranberries, raisins, and almonds while the cereal is still hot. Cool completely before storing.

nutrition info

*For **2 servings** each serving contains:*

Calories:	427
Fat:	16g
Protein:	10g
Cholesterol:	0mg
Carbohydrates:	68g
Sodium:	7mg

*For **3 servings** each serving contains:*

Calories:	285
Fat:	10g
Protein:	7g
Cholesterol:	0mg
Carbohydrates:	45g
Sodium:	4mg

blueberry buckwheat pancakes >>

nutrition info

*For **2 servings** each serving contains:*

Calories:	433
Fat:	6g
Protein:	20g
Cholesterol:	113mg
Carbohydrates:	81g
Sodium:	1350mg

*For **3 servings** each serving contains:*

Calories:	289
Fat:	4g
Protein:	13g
Cholesterol:	76mg
Carbohydrates:	54g
Sodium:	900 mg

Pancakes are really not just for Sunday breakfast. We love to eat them for dinner, especially after a cool day's hike in the Northwest woods.

¾ cup whole-wheat flour

½ cup buckwheat flour

2 tablespoons brown sugar

1 teaspoon baking powder

½ teaspoon baking soda

½ teaspoon salt

1⅔ cups buttermilk

1 large egg

1 tablespoon unsweetened applesauce

¼ cup water

1 cup blueberries, fresh or frozen and thawed

Pure maple syrup

1. In a medium bowl, stir together the dry ingredients. In a separate bowl, combine the buttermilk, egg, applesauce, and water and add to the flour mixture. Stir lightly until blended. If the consistency is too thick, add more water, 1 tablespoon at a time. Fold in blueberries.

2. Spoon ⅓ cup batter for each pancake onto a hot nonstick griddle or skillet. Flip the pancakes over when the surface bubbles and the edges are slightly dry. Cook until dark golden brown. Serve with maple syrup.

calzone >>

What a great idea—a pizza wrapped up to take on the road! You'll love this calzone at home or as a traveling meal.

3 teaspoons extra virgin olive oil

1 small eggplant, diced

1 tomato, diced

6 button mushrooms, sliced

1 scallion, sliced

1 teaspoon dried basil

1 teaspoon dried oregano

One 11-ounce package refrigerator dough (Pillsbury Crusty French Loaf)

½ cup nonfat ricotta cheese

⅛ cup freshly grated Parmesan cheese

¼ cup shredded low-fat mozzarella cheese

nutrition info

*For **2 servings** each serving contains:*

Calories:	737
Fat:	24g
Protein:	36g
Cholesterol:	37mg
Carbohydrates:	98g
Sodium:	1416mg

*For **3 servings** each serving contains:*

Calories:	491
Fat:	16g
Protein:	24g
Cholesterol:	25mg
Carbohydrates:	65g
Sodium:	944mg

1. Preheat the oven to 400°F. In a nonstick frying pan over medium heat, heat 1 teaspoon oil for 1 minute. Cook the eggplant, tomato, mushrooms, and scallion with the basil and oregano, stirring, until tender, for 3 to 5 minutes. Drain off any liquid.

2. Unroll the dough to form a single layer. Cut it into 3 or 4 equal pieces.

3. Combine the cheeses and place equal amounts in the center of each dough square. Spoon the vegetables over the cheese and fold the dough to cover the filling.

4. With your fingers, pinch the dough edges shut to seal in the filling. Brush with the remaining olive oil and bake for 25 to 30 minutes or until golden brown.

cheese strata >>

People of all ages, especially the chef, love a strata, a layered casserole using eggs, bread, and cheese. It's easy to make, looks great, and is a great way to get in a good dose of calcium. One-third of the recipe gives you half of your daily RDA for calcium.

No-stick cooking spray

2 ounces mushrooms, chopped

2 ounces shallots, chopped

2 tablespoons white wine

4 slices whole-wheat bread

4 ounces low-fat shredded cheddar cheese

2 eggs, beaten

1 cup 1-percent milk

1. Preheat the oven to 325°F.

2. Heat a skillet over high heat for 30 seconds. Spray the skillet and cook the mushrooms and onions, stirring, until soft, about 5 minutes. Add the wine and continue cooking for 3 minutes. Remove from the heat.

3. Cover the bottom of the loaf pan with 2 slices of bread. Sprinkle with half of the cheese and all of the sautéed vegetables.

4. Place the other 2 slices of bread on top of the cheeses and vegetables. Add the remaining cheeses.

5. Combine the eggs and milk. Pour over the bread and refrigerate for several hours or overnight to allow the milk to soak into the bread.

6. Bake for 45 minutes or until brown and bubbly.

nutrition info

For **2 servings** each serving contains:

Calories:	424
Fat:	13g
Protein:	31g
Cholesterol:	204mg
Carbohydrates:	46g
Sodium:	503mg

For **3 servings** each serving contains:

Calories:	283
Fat:	9g
Protein:	21g
Cholesterol:	136mg
Carbohydrates:	31g
Sodium:	335mg

corn soufflé >>

For a high-carb load without the obligatory pasta, try this corn dish. It is loaded with thiamin, niacin, riboflavin, folacin, calcium, and iron, as well as carbohydrates and fiber. This recipe can easily serve 6 to 8 for a light main dish.

No-stick cooking spray

One 8-ounce package corn bread mix

One 15-ounce can creamed corn

One 15-ounce can regular corn, undrained

4 egg whites

8 ounces low-fat plain yogurt

6 tablespoons unsalted butter

1. Preheat the oven to 350°F. Coat a 13 × 9-inch glass baking dish with cooking spray.

2. In a large bowl, combine the remaining ingredients, pour into the dish, and bake for 1 hour. Serve immediately.

nutrition info

For **6 servings** each serving contains:

Calories:	375
Fat:	14g
Protein:	11g
Cholesterol:	22mg
Carbohydrates:	54g
Sodium:	985mg

For **8 servings** each serving contains:

Calories:	281
Fat:	11g
Protein:	8g
Cholesterol:	16mg
Carbohydrates:	41g
Sodium:	739mg

chili corn cakes >>

Keka is a wonderful tapas restaurant in Ohio City, Cleveland. This dish is one of the favorites at the restaurant.

½ red bell pepper, minced

½ green bell pepper, minced

¼ red onion, peeled and minced

2 tablespoons canola oil

¾ cup frozen corn kernels, thawed

¼ teaspoon Tabasco or other hot sauce

⅛ teaspoon ground coriander

2 teaspoons mild paprika

¼ cup unbleached all-purpose flour

¾ teaspoon baking powder

¼ cup coarse yellow cornmeal

1 egg white

¼ cup skim milk

3 ounces soy or other vegetarian sausage

No-stick cooking spray

1. In a large skillet over medium heat, cook the peppers and onion in the oil until soft, about 5 minutes. Add the corn kernels and continue cooking for 3 minutes more. Mix in the Tabasco and set aside.

2. Combine the coriander, paprika, flour, baking powder, and cornmeal. Mix until blended. Add the vegetable mixture, egg white, and milk and stir until all ingredients are moistened. Set aside and let stand for 10 minutes.

3. In a nonstick skillet over medium heat, cook the sausage until brown, about 5 minutes. Meanwhile, heat another nonstick skillet over high heat for 30 seconds. Spray the skillet well with cooking spray. Spoon about ¼ cup of the batter onto the skillet and reduce the heat to medium. When air bubbles appear on the surface of each cake, after about 4 to 5 minutes, turn the cake over and cook the other side for 2 to 3 minutes more. Remove the cakes from the heat and continue until all the batter is used up.

4. Mince the cooked sausage and sprinkle on top of the chili corn cakes.

curried rice and chickpeas >>

Curried dishes are traditionally served with plain yogurt to offset the spicy heat of the curry. This recipe is light on the curry powder, so it is not so spicy. You can add more curry to suit your own tastes.

1¼ tablespoons safflower oil

½ medium onion, peeled and chopped

1 medium carrot, diced

½ cup frozen cut green beans

1 small potato, diced

1 teaspoon salt

⅛ teaspoon garlic powder

1 teaspoon curry powder

One 15-ounce can chickpeas, drained

½ cup cooked brown rice

⅓ cup water

Plain low-fat yogurt (optional)

1. Heat the oil in a nonstick skillet over medium-high heat. Add the onion and cook, stirring, for 2 minutes. Add the carrot, green beans, potato, salt, garlic powder, and curry powder, and cook, stirring, about 5 minutes more.

2. In a medium saucepan, combine the chickpeas, rice, cooked vegetables, and water. Simmer over low heat, covered, for 20 minutes or until the vegetables are tender. The cover may be removed toward the end of cooking to allow any extra liquid to boil off. Serve with or without yogurt on the side.

lentils with rice >>

Lentils were one of the first legumes cultivated and are mentioned in many ancient texts. This dish is a classic dish from the Middle East.

¾ cup lentils

¾ cup boiling water

2 tablespoons canola oil

1 large onion, peeled and chopped

1¼ cups brown rice

2 cups water

Salt and freshly ground black pepper to taste

1. Soak the lentils in boiling water for a minimum of 5 minutes or longer as needed.

2. Heat the canola oil in a saucepan over medium heat. Cook the onion in the canola oil until translucent, about 5 minutes.

3. Drain the lentils. Combine the lentils, rice, and water with the onion. Bring to a boil, reduce heat to low, cover the saucepan, and cook for 30 minutes or until the water is absorbed. Add salt and pepper.

nutrition info

*For **2 servings** each serving contains:*

Calories:	820
Fat:	18g
Protein:	30g
Cholesterol:	0mg
Carbohydrates:	137g
Sodium:	27mg

*For **3 servings** each serving contains:*

Calories:	547
Fat:	12g
Protein:	20g
Cholesterol:	0mg
Carbohydrates:	91g
Sodium:	18mg

111

marinated tofu and rice >>

This is the style of vegetarian cooking that I started with back in the 1970s. But the flavors are still great, and it remains one of my family's mainstay dishes.

1 tablespoon tamari sauce or regular soy sauce

1 teaspoon sesame oil

1 tablespoon rice vinegar (unseasoned)

2 teaspoons toasted sesame seeds (see note)

⅛ teaspoon ground ginger

½ teaspoon freshly ground black pepper

½ cup minced scallions

½ pound low-fat firm tofu, sliced into 1-inch cubes

No-stick cooking spray

1 teaspoon peanut oil

¼ red bell pepper, thinly sliced

2 cups cooked brown rice

1. In a bowl, mix together the soy sauce, sesame oil, rice vinegar, sesame seeds, ginger, black pepper, and scallions, and pour over the tofu. Let it marinate in the refrigerator for several hours.

2. Spray a nonstick skillet with cooking spray. Add the peanut oil and heat over medium-high heat. Add the red pepper and cook, stirring, for 30 seconds. Add the rice and cook, stirring, until heated through, about 5 minutes. Add the tofu and marinating liquid and heat until thoroughly warmed, about 3 minutes.

Note: To toast sesame seeds in a toaster oven, place them on the toaster oven tray, and set the oven on the lowest setting. Stir. If not totally toasted, repeat, but watch closely. To toast sesame seeds on the stove top, place them in a nonstick skillet over low heat, stirring frequently, for about 5 minutes.

marmaliga >>

This classic Hungarian polenta-like dish was my grand-mother's recipe, minus a whole lot of fat. A true Hungarian Rhapsody. (KFK)

3 cups water

1 cup coarse yellow cornmeal

½ teaspoon salt

1½ teaspoons unsalted butter

½ pound farmer's cheese

½ pound nonfat ricotta cheese

1. Preheat the oven to 350°F.

2. Combine 1 cup water and the cornmeal in an oven-safe frying pan or skillet. Mix thoroughly. Slowly add the remaining water to the cornmeal. Sprinkle the salt over the cornmeal and add the butter to the center of the skillet. Cover and cook over low heat for 20 to 25 minutes.

3. Combine the cheeses and spread them on top of the cornmeal. Transfer the skillet to the oven and bake uncovered for 10 minutes or until bubbly.

nutrition info

*For **2 servings** each serving contains:*

Calories:	808
Fat:	46g
Protein:	42g
Cholesterol:	144mg
Carbohydrates:	55g
Sodium:	2252mg

*For **3 servings** each serving contains:*

Calories:	539
Fat:	31g
Protein:	28g
Cholesterol:	96mg
Carbohydrates:	37g
Sodium:	1501mg

oatmeal banana pancakes >>

Why eat your old-fashioned oats in an old-fashioned bowl? These high-performance pancakes are a sure winner, especially when you're carbo loading.

1¼ cups buttermilk

½ cup rolled oats

½ teaspoon vanilla extract

1 tablespoon safflower oil

1 large egg

½ cup unbleached all-purpose flour

2 tablespoons brown sugar

½ teaspoon baking soda

½ teaspoon salt

1 cup mashed bananas (2 ripe bananas)

3 tablespoons chopped pecans

Pure maple syrup

1. In a small bowl, combine the buttermilk, oats, and vanilla. Stir and let stand for 10 minutes, stirring occasionally. Stir in the oil and egg.

2. In a large bowl, combine the flour, brown sugar, baking soda, and salt. Stir well. Add the oat mixture to the flour mixture and stir until smooth. Fold in the bananas and pecans.

3. Spoon ⅓ cup of batter for each pancake onto a hot nonstick griddle or skillet. Flip the pancakes over to cook the other side when the surface bubbles and the edges are slightly dry. Cook the pancakes until they are dark golden brown. Serve with maple syrup.

pina colada rice >>

With a green vegetable on the side, this dish serves as virtually a whole meal, dessert and all. You can grow your own pineapple sage and mint in an indoor herb garden. The leaves smell as great as they taste.

14 ounces (1¾ cups) vegetable broth (page 71)

2 cups instant brown rice

¼ cup sweetened shredded coconut

3 cups fresh pineapple, diced

2 tablespoons coconut milk

2 tablespoons rum (optional)

⅓ cup sugar

1 cup firm tofu, diced

2 tablespoons minced fresh pineapple sage or fresh mint

1. In a saucepan over high heat, bring the broth to a boil. Add the rice, coconut, pineapple, coconut milk, rum, and sugar. Cover, reduce the heat to low, and cook for 5 minutes.

2. Add the tofu and continue cooking, covered, for 4 more minutes. Add the pineapple sage and cook, covered, for 1 minute or until all of the liquid has been absorbed and the rice is tender. Toss to distribute the sage and serve.

nutrition info

*For **2 servings** each serving contains:*

Calories:	1148
Fat:	19g
Protein:	31g
Cholesterol:	0mg
Carbohydrates:	217g
Sodium:	541mg

*For **3 servings** each serving contains:*

Calories:	765
Fat:	13g
Protein:	21g
Cholesterol:	0mg
Carbohydrates:	144g
Sodium:	360mg

115

springtime rice pancake >>

nutrition info

For **2 servings** each serving contains:

Calories:	299
Fat:	10g
Protein:	21g
Cholesterol:	281mg
Carbohydrates:	31g
Sodium:	389mg

For **3 servings** each serving contains:

Calories:	199
Fat:	7g
Protein:	14g
Cholesterol:	187mg
Carbohydrates:	21g
Sodium:	259mg

This low-calorie pancake is reminiscent of the Chinese dish egg foo yong. Experiment with the ingredients by adding some of your own home-grown bean sprouts.

1 teaspoon peanut oil

2 ounces enoki mushrooms or mung bean sprouts

¼ cup frozen peas, thawed

2 scallions, sliced diagonally

2 teaspoons low-sodium soy sauce

1 cup cooked brown rice

3 whole medium eggs

4 medium egg whites

¼ cup alfalfa sprouts

1. In a nonstick wok or skillet over medium-high heat, heat the oil. Add the mushrooms, peas, and scallions, and cook, stirring, for 3 minutes. Add the soy sauce and stir. Add the rice and heat thoroughly.

2. Lightly beat eggs and egg whites together until foamy. Push the rice mixture to the sides of the skillet, making a well in the center. Pour the eggs into the well and let them start cooking. Carefully blend the rice mixture into the eggs and smooth into a large pancake. Continue cooking until the pancake is browned on the bottom, about 5 minutes. To serve, cut the pancake in half or in thirds. Garnish with the alfalfa sprouts.

thai basmati rice >>

A carbohydrate-lover's dream, this side dish is served hot but is also tasty cold and can even be sprinkled on a salad.

¼ cup sweetened shredded coconut

2 cups cooked basmati rice

Juice of ½ lime

In a nonstick skillet over medium-high heat, toast the coconut for about 1 minute, stirring frequently. Reduce the heat to medium and add the rice and lime juice. Mix thoroughly. Cook for another 5 minutes, stirring frequently.

nutrition info

For **2 servings** each serving contains:

Calories:	793
Fat:	7g
Protein:	16g
Cholesterol:	0mg
Carbohydrates:	169g
Sodium:	31mg

For **3 servings** each serving contains:

Calories:	529
Fat:	4g
Protein:	11g
Cholesterol:	0mg
Carbohydrates:	113g
Sodium:	20mg

tofu fried rice >>

This one-pot meal is a Chinese staple. It is densely packed with calories, carbohydrates, protein, vitamins, minerals, fiber, and phytochemicals.

nutrition info

*For **2 servings** each serving contains:*

Calories:	1177
Fat:	16g
Protein:	33g
Cholesterol:	187mg
Carbohydrates:	224g
Sodium:	457mg

*For **3 servings** each serving contains:*

Calories:	785
Fat:	11g
Protein:	22g
Cholesterol:	125mg
Carbohydrates:	150g
Sodium:	304mg

½ teaspoon peanut oil

2 garlic cloves, peeled and minced

1 medium carrot, scraped and diced

¼ cup frozen tiny green peas, thawed

⅓ cup scallions, sliced diagonally

3 ounces low-fat firm tofu, diced

3 cups cooked white or brown rice
(1½ cups raw)

2 teaspoons low-sodium soy sauce

2 large eggs, beaten

1. Heat oil in a nonstick wok over medium-high heat until hot. Add the garlic and stir-fry for 30 seconds. Add the carrot, green peas, scallions, and tofu, and cook, stirring, for 2 minutes. Add the rice and soy sauce, stirring until well heated.

2. Push the mixture to the sides of the pan, forming a well in the center. Pour the eggs into the well, and cook until set, stirring occasionally.

3. Stir the rice mixture into the eggs and mix well.

indian fried rice >>

This fragrant dish will be one of the most wonderful rice dishes that you've ever had. It contains the four Cs of Indian cooking: cardamom, cinnamon, cloves, and cumin. It is certainly one of our favorites.

1 tablespoon unsalted butter

1 tablespoon safflower oil

4 whole cardamom pods

One 1-inch cinnamon stick

4 whole cloves

¼ teaspoon cumin seeds

2 medium onions, peeled and thinly sliced

1 cup basmati rice, washed and drained

1¾ cups boiling water

½ teaspoon salt

1. In a skillet over medium-high heat, heat the butter and oil until the butter is melted. Add the cardamom, cinnamon, cloves, and cumin seeds, and cook, stirring, for 1 minute.

2. Add the onions and cook, stirring, until lightly browned, 5 to 7 minutes. Add the rice and cook, stirring frequently to prevent burning, until golden brown.

3. Add the water and salt and bring to a boil. Cover the skillet with a tight lid and reduce the heat to low. Cook for 10 minutes or until the water is absorbed. Remove from the heat and serve.

nutrition info

*For **2 servings** each serving contains:*

Calories:	597
Fat:	16g
Protein:	11g
Cholesterol:	16mg
Carbohydrates:	110g
Sodium:	622mg

*For **3 servings** each serving contains:*

Calories:	398
Fat:	11g
Protein:	7g
Cholesterol:	10mg
Carbohydrates:	74g
Sodium:	415mg

119

*bevy of
beans*

baked lentil pies >>

Lentils are a staple protein source for many cultures around the world. The combination of the lentils and the wheat pie crust creates a complete protein source. And the taste is fabulous.

baked lentil pie filling

¼ **cup lentils**

¾ **cup water**

1 **large hard-boiled egg**

½ **large onion, peeled and sliced**

¼ **tablespoon canola oil**

Salt and freshly ground black pepper to taste

pie crust

¾ **cup unbleached all-purpose flour**

½ **teaspoon baking powder**

¼ **teaspoon sugar**

⅛ **teaspoon salt**

2 **tablespoons unsalted butter, softened**

1 **egg white, beaten**

¾ **cup water**

---

nutrition info

For **2 servings** *each serving contains:*

Calories:	402
Fat:	14g
Protein:	16g
Cholesterol:	31mg
Carbohydrates:	54g
Sodium:	437mg

For **3 servings** *each serving contains:*

Calories:	268
Fat:	9g
Protein:	10g
Cholesterol:	21mg
Carbohydrates:	36g
Sodium:	291mg

1. Preheat the oven to 400°F.

2. For the filling, cook the lentils in the water in a large saucepan over medium-high heat until soft and all the water is absorbed, about 30 minutes.

3. Cut open the cooled egg and separate the yolk from the white. Discard the yolk.

4. In a skillet over medium-high heat, cook the onion in the oil until translucent, about 5 minutes.

5. Blend the lentils, egg white, onion, and salt and pepper in a blender or food processor until pastelike. Set aside.

6. For the crust, sift together the flour, baking powder, sugar, and salt in a large bowl. Add the butter and blend until mixture is crumbly. Add the egg white and water and mix together until a dough is formed.

7. Roll out the dough on a floured surface to ⅛ inch thick and place in a pie pan with the dough overlapping the sides. Fill with the lentil mixture. Fold dough on top of the pie. Brush with a beaten egg if desired.

8. Bake for 25 to 30 minutes or until brown.

bean and cheese
enchiladas >>

For **2 servings** each serving contains:

Calories:	681
Fat:	20g
Protein:	42g
Cholesterol:	25mg
Carbohydrates:	95g
Sodium:	1884mg

For **3 servings** each serving contains:

Calories:	454
Fat:	14g
Protein:	28g
Cholesterol:	17mg
Carbohydrates:	64g
Sodium:	1256mg

By using the new low-fat cheeses, we can re-create favorite high-fat dishes in a low-fat form. If you prefer, you can even eliminate the cheese here for a completely vegan dish. Select wheat tortillas made without lard; we prefer corn tortillas for enchiladas.

1 teaspoon safflower oil

1 small onion, peeled and diced

2 garlic cloves, peeled and minced

1 tablespoon diced green chilies, or more to taste

One 14½-ounce can chopped tomatoes

¾ cup tomato juice

¼ teaspoon dried basil

¾ cup low-sodium vegetable broth (page 71)

¾ tablespoon cornstarch, dissolved in 3 tablespoons cold water

One 15-ounce can pinto beans, pureed with can liquid

½ cup chili sauce

6 large corn or wheat tortillas

3 scallions, chopped

1¼ cups grated low-fat cheddar cheese

1. Preheat the oven to 350°F.

2. To prepare the sauce, place a large nonstick skillet over medium heat and add the oil. Add the onion and garlic and cook, stirring, until transparent, about 5 minutes. Add the chilies, tomatoes, tomato juice, and basil. Reduce the heat to low and cook about 6 minutes, then add the vegetable broth and cornstarch. Stir well and cook for another 10 minutes, uncovered, stirring occasionally. Let sit over low heat.

3. To prepare the filling, in a bowl, combine the pureed beans with the chili sauce.

4. Heat a skillet over medium-high heat. Place one tortilla at a time in the skillet. When the tortilla is warmed and soft (about 30 to 45 seconds), carefully remove it from the skillet and place it on top of the warm sauce in the other skillet. Carefully lift the tortilla from the sauce (a thin layer of sauce should be clinging to the tortilla), and flip it so the sauce side faces up. Spoon a generous portion of the bean mixture, chopped scallions, and cheese onto the tortilla. Roll up the tortilla and place it on a baking sheet. Repeat the process for the remaining tortillas.

5. Pour the remaining sauce over the tortillas. Bake for 15 minutes. Serve hot.

baked beans >>

When we stop buying canned vegetables, we often forget about this American classic. But baked beans are great not only at picnics and barbecues; you can enjoy them year-round.

6 tablespoons low-sodium tomato paste

1 teaspoon prepared yellow mustard

½ teaspoon minced garlic

2 tablespoons red wine

2 tablespoons low-sodium soy sauce

⅓ cup pure maple syrup

1 teaspoon balsamic vinegar

One 15-ounce can pinto beans, drained

1. Combine all the ingredients except the beans in a large pot. Mix until smooth. Cook over medium heat until the mixture bubbles.

2. Add the beans and cook for 10 minutes. Remove from the heat and serve.

nutrition info

For 2 servings each serving contains:

Calories:	383
Fat:	2g
Protein:	13g
Cholesterol:	0mg
Carbohydrates:	77g
Sodium:	490mg

For 3 servings each serving contains:

Calories:	255
Fat:	1g
Protein:	9g
Cholesterol:	0mg
Carbohydrates:	52g
Sodium:	327mg

bean and pasta salad >>

I love to take this salad to potluck dinners. It's fast and easy, it doesn't require refrigeration, and I'm assured a good plant protein source if only meat is being served. (SMK)

1½ cups tricolor bow-tie pasta

¾ cup green beans, fresh or frozen

¼ cup extra virgin olive oil

¼ cup cider vinegar

1 tablespoon sugar

½ teaspoon salt

1 teaspoon chopped fresh parsley

½ teaspoon celery seed

6 ounces canned red kidney beans, drained (⅔ cup)

1 small onion, thinly sliced

½ cup chopped red bell pepper

¼ cup chopped yellow bell pepper

nutrition info

For **2 servings** each serving contains:

Calories:	507
Fat:	17g
Protein:	16g
Cholesterol:	0mg
Carbohydrates:	75g
Sodium:	487mg

For **3 servings** each serving contains:

Calories:	338
Fat:	11g
Protein:	11g
Cholesterol:	0mg
Carbohydrates:	50g
Sodium:	324mg

1. Cook the pasta according to package directions, about 12 minutes. Drain and cool. Cook the green beans for just a few minutes in simmering water until they are barely done. Drain and cool the beans.

2. In a carafe or dressing container, mix together the oil, vinegar, sugar, salt, parsley, and celery seed. In a salad bowl, combine the pasta, green beans, kidney beans, onion, and bell peppers. Pour the dressing over the salad and marinate it at least 1 hour or overnight, refrigerated.

sprout salad >>

Many Asian cultures use mung bean sprouts as a major ingredient in salads. By sprouting your own beans and seeds, you can always create a new mixture for this light and tasty salad.

2 cups mung bean sprouts

1 cup mixed sprouts: alfalfa, safflower, cabbage, lentil

6 tablespoons shredded daikon radish

1 cup very thinly sliced English cucumber

1 cup shredded red cabbage

1 teaspoon minced fresh cilantro

½ tablespoon toasted sesame seeds (page 112)

2 to 3 tablespoons rice vinegar

In a salad bowl, mix together the sprouts, daikon, cucumber, cabbage, cilantro, and sesame seeds. Sprinkle with vinegar and let sit for 10 minutes. Serve.

choley >>

*This dish is often served with deep-fried bread called
Bhatoore. The chickpeas, or choley, are cream colored and
larger in size than the yellow chickpeas we usually buy in the
United States. They can be obtained from an Indian grocer.*

1 pound choley or dried white chickpeas

¼ teaspoon ground turmeric

1¼ teaspoons salt

1 tablespoon corn oil

**2 small onions, peeled, one diced and one
chopped**

¼ teaspoon cumin seeds

1 whole cardamom pod

½ cup water

¼ teaspoon garlic powder

1 tablespoon ground coriander

¼ teaspoon ground ginger

⅛ teaspoon freshly ground black pepper

1 firm tomato, chopped

2 tablespoons chopped fresh cilantro leaves

3 large pita circles, toasted

nutrition info

*For 2 servings each serving
contains:*

Calories:	1112
Fat:	23g
Protein:	52g
Cholesterol:	0mg
Carbohydrates:	185g
Sodium:	1758mg

*For 3 servings each serving
contains:*

Calories:	741
Fat:	15g
Protein:	35g
Cholesterol:	0mg
Carbohydrates:	123g
Sodium:	1172mg

1. Soak the *choley* in water to cover overnight. The next day add the
turmeric and ½ teaspoon salt and cook in a covered saucepan over high
heat until softened, about 30 minutes. Alternatively, use a pressure
cooker and cook for 5 minutes.

2. Meanwhile, in a skillet over medium heat, add the oil and cook the diced
onion with the cumin seeds and cardamom, stirring, until the onion is
light brown, about 5 minutes.

3. Add the water, remaining salt, and spices. Cook, stirring, until the water
evaporates and the oil separates from the mixture, about 20 minutes.

4. Mix the onion mixture with the choley, and add the chopped raw onion
and tomato. Sprinkle with cilantro and serve with the toasted pita.

129

edamame >>

This is a very traditional Japanese dish, often served at sushi bars. You might notice that there is a higher percentage of fat in the analysis for this recipe than in our other recipes. Since this is the natural amount of oil found in soybeans, and soybeans are such an incredibly healthful food, we feel that they play an important role in the vegetarian diet despite their high fat content. Frozen soybeans can be purchased at most Asian food markets.

1 pound frozen soybeans in the hull

2 quarts boiling water

½ tablespoon coarse salt or sea salt

In a large saucepan, cook the soybeans in boiling water for 3 minutes. Drain and rinse under cold running water. Sprinkle with salt to taste. Serve warm or cold in the hull. Remove the hull to eat the soybeans inside.

nutrition info

*For **2 servings** each serving contains:*

Calories:	392
Fat:	20g
Protein:	38g
Cholesterol:	0mg
Carbohydrates:	23g
Sodium:	564mg

*For **3 servings** each serving contains:*

Calories:	262
Fat:	14g
Protein:	25g
Cholesterol:	0mg
Carbohydrates:	15g
Sodium:	376mg

falafel salad >>

Falafel patties are traditionally deep fried. This recipe creates a superb, low-fat rendition, and then marries the Middle Eastern flavors with some American Southwestern flair.

One 15-ounce can chickpeas, drained

1 teaspoon garlic powder

2 tablespoons water

1 teaspoon paprika

1 tablespoon canola oil

6 ounces spinach, washed and shredded

1 grapefruit, peeled and diced

½ jicama, julienned

Harissa (page 61)

1. In a food processor or blender, combine the beans, garlic powder, water, and paprika. Process until a crumbly paste forms.

2. Heat a nonstick skillet over medium heat for 30 seconds. Add the oil and heat for 1 minute, until hot.

3. Form the chickpea mixture into small patties, using about 1 tablespoon mixture for each. Place in the oil. Cook on medium-high for 3 to 5 minutes, or until light brown. Turn over the patties and cook until the second side turns light brown. Drain on paper towels. Repeat with remaining mixture.

4. Place the spinach on individual plates. Top with grapefruit and jicama. Place the warm patties on the salad and serve with Harissa.

nutrition info

For **2 servings** each serving contains:

Calories:	377
Fat:	10g
Protein:	14g
Cholesterol:	0mg
Carbohydrates:	61g
Sodium:	928mg

For **3 servings** each serving contains:

Calories:	251
Fat:	7g
Protein:	10g
Cholesterol:	0mg
Carbohydrates:	41g
Sodium:	618mg

131

fava beans in
wine sauce >>

Fava beans prepared this way are a traditional dish of Italy. While fresh fava beans can be found in the open-air markets of Rome, it is easier to get them at your local specialty store, even if it's not as romantic!

25 fava bean pods (see note)

1 cup water

2 shallots, peeled and sliced

2 garlic cloves, peeled and sliced

2 teaspoons olive oil

¼ cup white wine

1. Microwave the beans in the water on high for 10 minutes in a covered, microwave-safe dish.

2. Meanwhile, in a skillet over high heat, cook the shallots and garlic in the oil, stirring, for 5 minutes. Add the wine and reduce the heat to low.

3. Peel the fava bean pods and place the beans into the pan with the garlic and onions. Continue to cook, stirring, for 5 minutes and serve.

Note: Fava beans can be purchased seasonally at farmer's markets or specialty food stores. Frozen or canned beans are not a suitable substitute. Blanching the beans first may make removing the skins easier.

green and
bean salad >>

If you love Salade Nicoise, but don't eat fish anymore, try this salad. It will remind you of the tastes that you've been missing.

6 small red potatoes, washed, halved, and cooked

One 8-ounce bag prewashed salad greens

⅔ cup chickpeas

2 thin slices red onion

6 cherry tomatoes, halved

8 slices cucumber

2 large mushrooms, sliced

6 fresh parsley sprigs

4 ounces low-fat firm tofu, cubed

½ cup alfalfa sprouts

heritage *dressing*

3 tablespoons extra virgin olive oil

¼ cup red wine vinegar

3 tablespoons water

1¼ teaspoons garlic powder

⅛ teaspoon white pepper, or freshly ground black pepper

½ teaspoon dried basil

½ teaspoon vegetable-seasoning salt (such as Vegesal)

1 tablespoon freshly grated Parmesan cheese

nutrition info

For **2 servings** each serving contains:

Calories:	684
Fat:	24g
Protein:	29g
Cholesterol:	39mg
Carbohydrates:	93g
Sodium:	800mg

For **3 servings** each serving contains:

Calories:	456
Fat:	16g
Protein:	19g
Cholesterol:	26mg
Carbohydrates:	62g
Sodium:	533mg

1. In a large serving bowl, combine the salad ingredients.

2. In a small bowl or dressing container, combine the dressing ingredients. Pour over the salad and toss to combine well.

133

huevos rancheros >>

Breakfast, lunch, or dinner, this Mexican favorite is packed with iron, high-quality protein, and lots of fiber.

2 or 3 corn tortillas

2 teaspoons corn oil

4 large eggs

1 cup Refried Beans (page 136), warmed

½ cup low-fat shredded cheddar cheese

⅔ cup salsa

1. Brush each tortilla with oil. Place each tortilla, oil side down, in a nonstick skillet and heat over medium heat until warmed and crisp, about 2 minutes. Remove tortillas and set aside. Fry the eggs in the same skillet, sunny-side up, until firm.

2. Meanwhile, place some of the refried beans on each tortilla. Top the beans with the eggs and shredded cheese.

3. Spoon the salsa over the eggs and serve.

molletes >>

If you are looking for real Mexican food, this is it.

2 large hamburger buns or 3 medium rolls

½ cup Refried Beans (page 136)

1 cup shredded low-fat cheddar cheese

¼ cup salsa

1. Slice the buns in half lengthwise.

2. Spread the rolls with refried beans. Top with cheese.

3. Broil for 4 to 5 minutes until the cheese has melted. Top each sandwich with salsa and serve.

nutrition info

*For **2 servings** each serving contains:*

Calories:	270
Fat:	7g
Protein:	19g
Cholesterol:	12mg
Carbohydrates:	30g
Sodium:	688mg

*For **3 servings** each serving contains:*

Calories:	180
Fat:	4g
Protein:	13g
Cholesterol:	8mg
Carbohydrates:	20g
Sodium:	458mg

refried beans >>

Traditionally, refried beans are made with lard. These are healthier, and without the lard, they're vegetarian, too. They can be eaten as a main dish or incorporated into dishes like Molletes and Huevos Rancheros.

nutrition info

For **2 servings** each serving contains:

Calories:	252
Fat:	9g
Protein:	12g
Cholesterol:	0mg
Carbohydrates:	31g
Sodium:	440mg

For **3 servings** each serving contains:

Calories:	168
Fat:	6g
Protein:	8g
Cholesterol:	0mg
Carbohydrates:	21g
Sodium:	293mg

1½ tablespoons canola oil

One 15-ounce can pinto beans, drained

1 cup water

Salt to taste

1. In a skillet over high heat, warm the oil. Place the beans into the skillet. With a large spoon, mash the beans.

2. Add the water, as needed, to prevent burning. Stir frequently. Add salt to taste.

rotini fagioli >>

Beans are a wonderful source of the phytochemicals that are so protective against illness. This traditional bean and pasta combination is a staple of the Italian diet.

8 ounces tricolor vegetable rotini

One 19-ounce can black beans, drained

One 28-ounce can peeled tomatoes, drained and quartered

3 cups water

2 tablespoons low sodium vegetable-flavored bouillon (such as Better Than Bouillon)

1 tablespoon extra virgin olive oil

1 tablespoon lemon-herb seasoning

2 tablespoons fresh lemon juice

1. Combine all the ingredients except the lemon juice in a large saucepan. Bring to a boil over high heat. Reduce the heat to low, cover, and cook for 10 minutes. Stir occasionally to prevent sticking.

2. Check the pasta for desired doneness. If the water has been absorbed and you want your pasta softer, add an additional ¼ to ½ cup of water and continue cooking until the water is absorbed.

3. Toss the pasta mixture with the lemon juice and serve immediately.

nutrition info

*For **2 servings** each serving contains:*

Calories:	785
Fat:	16g
Protein:	35g
Cholesterol:	141mg
Carbohydrates:	128g
Sodium:	3665mg

*For **3 servings** each serving contains:*

Calories:	524
Fat:	11g
Protein:	23g
Cholesterol:	94mg
Carbohydrates:	85g
Sodium:	2443mg

succotash soufflé >>

For those unfamiliar with the dish, succotash is a mixture of lima beans and corn. And if you've never made a soufflé before, don't let it scare you. It's incredibly easy. Just don't keep opening and closing the oven door to check it while baking. That will certainly make it fall.

1 tablespoon unsalted butter

2 cups nonfat milk

½ cup coarse yellow cornmeal

3 large eggs, separated

1 cup frozen succotash, thawed

¾ teaspoon salt

Pinch cream of tartar

1. Preheat the oven to 400°F. Grease a soufflé dish with half the butter and set aside.

2. In a saucepan over medium-low heat, slowly bring the milk to a gentle boil. Stir in the remaining butter and the cornmeal. Continue cooking and stirring until the mixture is thick. Cool until lukewarm.

3. Beat the egg yolks into the cornmeal mixture, and fold in the succotash.

4. In a large bowl, whip the egg whites separately with the salt and cream of tartar until they form stiff peaks. Carefully fold them into the cornmeal mixture. Pile the mixture into the prepared soufflé dish and bake for 40 minutes. Serve at once.

tempeh salad
pita >>

This is such an appetizing way to add more soy to your diet. Even your nonvegetarian friends will ask for the recipe.

6 ounces tempeh

1 celery stalk, minced

2 tablespoons minced dill pickle

2 tablespoons minced onion

2 tablespoons minced fresh parsley

2 tablespoons chopped pecans

¼ cup nonfat mayonnaise

1 teaspoon prepared mustard

1 teaspoon soy sauce

Dash garlic powder

Freshly ground black pepper

Romaine lettuce leaves

2 or 3 whole-wheat pita pockets

1. Steam the tempeh for 20 minutes. Cool and cut into ⅜-inch cubes.

2. In a large bowl, mix together all the ingredients except the lettuce and the bread. Place some of the salad and lettuce in each pita pocket and enjoy.

nutrition info

For 2 servings each serving contains:

Calories:	370
Fat:	13g
Protein:	22g
Cholesterol:	0mg
Carbohydrates:	47g
Sodium:	599mg

For 3 servings each serving contains:

Calories:	247
Fat:	9g
Protein:	15g
Cholesterol:	0mg
Carbohydrates:	31g
Sodium:	400mg

tofu pineapple
salad >>

Tofu really takes on the taste of the tropics when it is combined with pineapple. Try to get fresh tofu—eaten raw, fresh tofu is far superior to packaged brands. Remember, sprouts need only to be rinsed and they make an easy salad addition. Most of the nutritional value is in the tiny nut-textured hulls, so do not remove them.

3 cups bean sprouts

1 medium onion, peeled and diced

1 cup sliced zucchini (one 6-inch zucchini)

1 cup sliced carrots (2 medium carrots)

¾ cup pineapple chunks in natural juice, drained

1 cup diced tofu (½-inch chunks)

2 teaspoons extra virgin olive oil

½ teaspoon garlic powder

3 slices whole-wheat bread

2 tablespoons freshly grated Parmesan cheese

dressing

3 tablespoons canola oil

¼ cup minced scallions

1 tablespoon minced garlic

1 tablespoon balsamic vinegar

½ teaspoon honey

2 tablespoons light soy sauce

2 tablespoons water

1 tablespoon marsala wine

⅛ teaspoon cayenne pepper

1. Toss the sprouts, onion, zucchini, carrots, pineapple, and tofu until well mixed. Set aside.

2. Combine the olive oil and garlic powder. Remove the crust from the bread. Spread the oil on the bread and sprinkle with Parmesan cheese. Toast the bread in a toaster oven and cut it into $\frac{1}{2}$-inch squares.

3. Toss the toast with the vegetables.

4. For the dressing, heat a skillet over low heat and add the oil. Add the scallions and garlic and cook, stirring, for 5 minutes. Add the vinegar, honey, soy sauce, water, wine, and pepper to the skillet. Mix thoroughly, and serve warm over the vegetables.

traveling noodle casserole >>

I have made this casserole since beginning my doctoral work. It was great for dinner, and the leftovers, packed in a plastic container, made a great lunch the next day, as I traveled on the road to meet research subjects and collect their dietary data. (SMK)

1 tablespoon peanut oil

½ tablespoon minced fresh ginger

2 garlic cloves, peeled and minced

½ large onion, peeled and sliced

1 medium zucchini, sliced

1 medium yellow squash, sliced

1 cup sliced mushrooms

1 tablespoon low-sodium soy sauce

6 ounces dry wide, flat whole-wheat noodles, cooked

½ pound low-fat firm tofu, crumbled

1 cup low-fat shredded mozzarella cheese (4 ounces)

½ cup freshly shredded or grated Parmesan cheese

1. Preheat the oven to 375°F.

2. Heat the oil in a nonstick skillet over medium-high heat. Add the ginger and garlic and cook for 30 seconds. Add the onion, zucchini and yellow squash. Cook, stirring, for 2 minutes. Add the mushrooms and cook, stirring, another 1 to 2 minutes. Add the soy sauce and mix well.

3. Combine the noodles, vegetable mixture, tofu, and mozzarella in a 2-quart casserole dish. Mix well and top with Parmesan cheese. Cover and bake for 15 minutes. Uncover and broil for 4 to 5 minutes to brown the cheese. Watch closely to avoid burning.

white chili >>

When dreaming of a white Christmas, have some White Chili! This unusual variation of chili is packed with fiber, phytoestrogens, potassium, and iron.

1 bunch scallions, minced (1 cup)

½ tablespoon extra virgin olive oil

½ red bell pepper, chopped

2 garlic cloves, minced

½ jalapeño chili, seeded and finely chopped

2 ounces canned mild green chilies, drained and diced

½ tablespoon ground cumin

⅛ cup fresh oregano, chopped

⅛ teaspoon ground cloves

¼ teaspoon cayenne pepper

8 ounces dried Great Northern beans, soaked overnight (or 24 ounces canned)

1 cup vegetable broth (page 71)

12 ounces beer

1 pound low-fat firm tofu, cubed

1 cup low-fat shredded mozzarella cheese

Salt and freshly ground black pepper to taste

Chopped fresh cilantro

nutrition info

For **2 servings** each serving contains:

Calories:	929
Fat:	26g
Protein:	67g
Cholesterol:	31mg
Carbohydrates:	100g
Sodium:	978mg

For **3 servings** each serving contains:

Calories:	619
Fat:	17g
Protein:	45g
Cholesterol:	20mg
Carbohydrates:	66g
Sodium:	652mg

1. In a skillet over medium heat, cook the scallions in the oil, stirring, until softened, about 1 minute. Add the pepper, garlic, chilies, cumin, oregano, cloves, and cayenne pepper, and cook, stirring, an additional 2 minutes.

2. Add the beans, broth, and beer and bring to a boil. Reduce the heat to low and cook until the beans are tender, about 20 minutes. Stir frequently.

3. Add the tofu and cheese and stir until the cheese is melted. Add salt and pepper. Garnish with chopped cilantro.

143

pasta
passion

acini di pepe >>

Acini di pepe *is a small, rice-shaped pasta often used in soups. Here we use it differently. It makes an excellent carbohydrate and electrolyte replacer.*

nutrition info

For **2 servings** each serving contains:

Calories:	899
Fat:	11g
Protein:	33g
Cholesterol:	0mg
Carbohydrates:	148g
Sodium:	996mg

For **3 servings** each serving contains:

Calories:	599
Fat:	8g
Protein:	22g
Cholesterol:	0mg
Carbohydrates:	98g
Sodium:	664mg

1 tablespoon extra virgin olive oil

1 garlic clove

1 cup uncooked acini di pepe

1 small onion, peeled and diced

6 mushrooms, sliced

½ cup chopped carrots

½ cup chopped parsley

1 cup white wine

1 cup vegetable broth (page 71)

6 ounces tomato paste

1. In a skillet, heat the olive oil over medium heat for 1 minute. Add the whole garlic clove and cook, stirring, for 2 minutes; remove the garlic and discard. In a separate pot, boil the *acini* pasta about 10 minutes until cooked.

2. Add the onion, mushrooms, carrots, and parsley to the skillet and cook, stirring, over medium heat until tender, about 5 to 7 minutes. Add the wine, broth, and tomato paste, and bring to a boil. Cook for 5 minutes.

3. Add the *acini de pepe* and stir until it is evenly coated. Serve hot.

baked ravioli >>

When time is really short and you need inspirational, fast food, turn frozen ravioli into a culinary delight in about 15 minutes.

10 sun-dried tomatoes

10 dried porcini mushrooms

1 tablespoon extra virgin olive oil

1 teaspoon garlic, peeled and chopped

¼ cup madeira wine

2 tablespoons pure maple syrup

6 ounces tomato paste

½ cup water

½ pound frozen cheese ravioli, cooked

¼ cup freshly grated Parmesan cheese

1. Preheat the oven to 350°F.

2. Soak the tomatoes and mushrooms in boiling water for 5 minutes. Drain and coarsely chop.

3. In a skillet over low heat, heat the oil and cook the garlic, stirring, for 1 minute. Add the chopped tomatoes and mushrooms to the garlic and cook, stirring, briefly.

4. In a small bowl, combine the wine, syrup, tomato paste, and water. Mix thoroughly and pour into the pan with the tomatoes and mushrooms. Cook, stirring, over medium heat for 5 minutes.

5. Layer half the ravioli in an oven-safe casserole and pour half the sauce over it. Sprinkle with half the cheese. Layer the remaining ravioli in the casserole and cover with the remaining sauce and cheese. Bake for 15 to 20 minutes until cheese begins to brown.

nutrition info

*For **2 servings** each serving contains:*

Calories:	750
Fat:	29g
Protein:	37g
Cholesterol:	120mg
Carbohydrates:	86g
Sodium:	1610mg

*For **3 servings** each serving contains:*

Calories:	500
Fat:	19g
Protein:	24g
Cholesterol:	80mg
Carbohydrates:	58g
Sodium:	1073mg

count basil spaetzle >>

nutrition info

For 2 servings each serving contains:

Calories:	487
Fat:	13g
Protein:	13g
Cholesterol:	0mg
Carbohydrates:	73g
Sodium:	310mg

For 3 servings each serving contains:

Calories:	325
Fat:	9g
Protein:	8g
Cholesterol:	0mg
Carbohydrates:	49g
Sodium:	207mg

Basil Spaetzle sounds like a German Count inspecting his fiefdom overlooking the Rhine. Spaetzle, a German noodle, is softer than most pasta. This version makes a main course or a wonderful accompaniment to other foods.

1 cup pasta flour or high-gluten semolina flour

2 teaspoons extra virgin olive oil

1 teaspoon chopped garlic

2 teaspoons fresh chopped basil

Dash salt

¼ cup hot water

basil spaetzle sauce

1 tablespoon extra virgin olive oil

1 teaspoon minced garlic

1 onion, peeled and chopped

4 ounces mushrooms, sliced

1 cup vegetable broth (page 71)

⅓ cup marsala wine or dry sherry

1 teaspoon cornstarch mixed with 2 table-spoons cold water

1. Place the pasta flour in a large bowl and make a well in the center.

2. Put the oil, garlic, and basil into the well. Add a dash of salt. Slowly add the water while adding the flour from the sides of the bowl into the well, stirring to mix with a fork.

3. When a soft ball forms, knead it 10 times, adding more flour as needed. Let the dough rest for 1 hour.

4. Roll out the dough on a floured surface into a thin sheet, about ⅛ inch thick, and slice into noodles about 2 inches long. Alternatively, use a pasta extruder.

5. Bring a saucepan of salted water to a boil and add the spaetzle. Cook for 5 minutes or until tender.

6. For the pasta sauce, in a large skillet over medium heat warm the olive oil for 1 minute. Add the garlic and onion and cook, stirring, until the onion is transluscent, about 5 minutes. Add the mushrooms and continue to cook, stirring, for 5 minutes.

7. Add the broth, wine, and cornstarch mixture and cook until thickened. Serve over spaetzle.

champagne-portobello farfalle >>

The name Champagne-Portobello Farfalle tickles the fancy while the food tickles your tastebuds, just like the leftover champagne. The champagne offers a unique flavor to this classic Italian dish.

2 tablespoons extra virgin olive oil

1 teaspoon minced garlic

3 portobello mushrooms, diced

6 button mushrooms, diced

4 sun-dried tomatoes, soaked in boiling water for 5 minutes to soften, minced

1 tablespoon all-purpose flour

⅛ cup freshly grated Parmesan cheese

½ cup skim milk

½ cup champagne

8 ounces dried farfalle pasta, cooked according to package directions

1. In a skillet over medium heat, heat the oil. Add the garlic and cook, stirring, for 1 minute. Add both the mushrooms and the tomatoes. Continue to cook, stirring, until the mushrooms are cooked, about 3 to 5 minutes.

2. Sprinkle the flour and cheese over the mushrooms, stirring to prevent clumping. Add the milk and champagne and continue cooking until sauce thickens, about 3 to 5 minutes. Serve over the pasta.

high-powered
COUSCOUS >>

Treat yourself to this one-bowl, high-carbohydrate vegetarian delight. Traditionally, a North African condiment called harissa, made with hot peppers, is used to dress the couscous. We have created our own, easily prepared version of harissa (page 61). For harissa aficionados, this is not completely authentic, but it makes for a quick and savory couscous dish.

¾ cup whole-wheat couscous

1½ cups boiling water

Salt to taste

1½ tablespoons extra virgin olive oil

1 teaspoon ground cinnamon

Dash white pepper

½ teaspoon ground cloves

2 medium carrots, cut into chunks

1 medium zucchini, cut into chunks

1 small parsnip, cut into chunks

1 ounce sun-dried tomatoes (about 10 tomatoes)

½ small yam, peeled and cut into chunks

1 small onion, peeled and cut into chunks

1 cup canned, drained chickpeas

Harissa (page 61)

nutrition info

For **2 servings** each serving contains:

Calories:	474
Fat:	14g
Protein:	13g
Cholesterol:	0mg
Carbohydrates:	80g
Sodium:	620mg

For **3 servings** each serving contains:

Calories:	316
Fat:	9g
Protein:	8g
Cholesterol:	0mg
Carbohydrates:	53g
Sodium:	413mg

1. Line a vegetable steamer with cheesecloth and set aside. In a heatproof bowl, combine the couscous, boiling water, and salt. Soak the couscous for 15 minutes. Pour off any remaining water and rub grains with your fingers to eliminate lumps. Stir in the oil, cinnamon, white pepper, and cloves.

2. Spread the couscous in cheesecloth-lined steamer over boiling water. Arrange the vegetables and chickpeas over the couscous. Cover and steam for 30 minutes or until the vegetables are done and the couscous is tender. Serve with warmed Harissa on the side.

151

marco polo orzo >>

Pasta originated in China and was brought back to Italy by Marco Polo. This dish combines traditional Chinese vegetables with a Mediterranean pasta treat. The mango, while not one of the fruits brought back to Italy by Marco Polo, provides beta-carotene for a high-antioxidant bonus.

nutrition info

*For **2 servings** each serving contains:*

Calories:	1286
Fat:	12g
Protein:	41g
Cholesterol:	0mg
Carbohydrates:	245g
Sodium:	187mg

*For **3 servings** each serving contains:*

Calories:	857
Fat:	8g
Protein:	27g
Cholesterol:	0mg
Carbohydrates:	163g
Sodium:	124mg

¼ cup sugar

¼ cup hoisin sauce

½ cup rice wine

2 garlic cloves, peeled and minced

3 slices ginger, approximately ⅛ inch thick, peeled and minced

1 tablespoon extra virgin olive oil

2 small Oriental eggplants, diced

1 mango, peeled and cut into ½-inch cubes

2 cups snowpeas

4 ounces shiitake mushrooms, sliced

8 ounces orzo (small rice-shaped pasta), cooked according to package directions

3 scallions, chopped

1. In a bowl, combine the sugar, hoisin sauce, rice wine, garlic, and ginger and mix until well blended. Set aside.

2. In a large pot, heat the olive oil over medium heat until hot, about 2 minutes. Add the eggplants, mango, snowpeas, and mushrooms and cook, stirring, for 5 minutes.

3. Add the orzo and the hoisin sauce mixture and mix thoroughly. Continue cooking over medium heat for 10 minutes or until the vegetables are tender. Stir the scallions into the mixture and serve immediately.

mushroom
kugel >>

From the same dictionary that gave you bobke, here's
kugel, an Eastern European pudding that can be sweet or
savory. It is made with noodles, potatoes, rice, or bread.
This version is a classic savory noodle version and an
excellent carbohydrate load.

2 tablespoons safflower oil

1 cup diced leeks

1 small onion, peeled and diced

6 large mushrooms, sliced

**⅓ pound fine egg noodles, cooked according to
package direction**

2 large eggs, beaten

½ teaspoon salt

¼ teaspoon freshly ground black pepper

1. Preheat the oven to 400°F.

2. Pour the oil into a 2-quart oven-safe casserole. Add the leeks, onion, and mushrooms.
Heat in the oven until hot, about 5 minutes.
Combine the remaining ingredients in a large
mixing bowl.

3. Remove the casserole from the oven and
carefully rock it back and forth to spread the
oil over the entire surface. Add the noodle
mixture and mix thoroughly. Bake for
30 minutes.

Note: *You can reduce the cholesterol and fat by removing
the yolks and adding 2 egg whites.*

nutrition info

For **2 servings** each serving
contains:

Calories:	1159
Fat:	29g
Protein:	41g
Cholesterol:	437mg
Carbohydrates:	182g
Sodium:	657mg

For **3 servings** each serving
contains:

Calories:	772
Fat:	19g
Protein:	27g
Cholesterol:	291mg
Carbohydrates:	122g
Sodium:	439mg

pasta alla fungi
e carciofani >>

It is hard to believe that a dish with such a romantic name can be so good for you. It is an excellent source of phytochemicals like lycopene and a great glycogen-loader at the same time.

1 tablespoon canola oil

1 teaspoon garlic, peeled and minced

One 14-ounce can artichoke hearts, drained and diced

5 plum tomatoes, peeled, seeded, and diced (see note)

8 porcini mushrooms, sliced

1 teaspoon minced fresh basil

1 teaspoon minced fresh oregano

One 16-ounce can tomato sauce

½ cup burgundy wine

8 ounces dried pasta, cooked according to package directions

1. In a large skillet, heat canola oil over medium heat for 1 minute. Add the garlic and cook, stirring, for a minute.

2. Add the artichoke hearts, tomatoes, mushrooms, basil, and oregano. Cook, stirring, for 10 minutes. Add the tomato sauce and wine and simmer for 20 minutes to blend the flavors and reduce the liquid. Serve over the pasta of your choice.

Note: *To peel tomatoes, plunge them into boiling water for about 1 minute. Remove immediately. The skins will peel off easily.*

porcini fungi
alla gorgonzola >>

The woody flavor of the mushrooms and walnuts contrasts well with the sharp taste of the gorgonzola cheese.

½ ounce dried porcini mushrooms

1½ cups low-sodium vegetable broth (page 71)

2 garlic cloves, peeled and minced

3 tablespoons chopped shallot (1 shallot)

½ ounce sun-dried tomatoes, chopped

¼ teaspoon salt

6 ounces dried angel-hair pasta

2 tablespoons chopped walnuts

3 ounces crumbled gorgonzola cheese

Freshly ground black pepper to taste

1. Clean any yellowish green spores from the mushrooms. Add ¼ cup of vegetable broth to a nonstick skillet and heat over medium-high heat for 1 minute. Add the garlic and shallot. Cover and cook for 2 minutes. Add the mushrooms, tomatoes, salt, and remaining vegetable broth. Bring to a boil, reduce the heat to low, and cook, uncovered, for 5 minutes.

2. Time the cooking of the pasta so that it is still hot when the sauce is ready.

3. Add the walnuts and crumbled gorgonzola to the sauce and stir well. Pour the sauce over the pasta. Sprinkle generously with freshly ground black pepper and toss before serving.

nutrition info

For **2 servings** each serving contains:

Calories:	621
Fat:	20g
Protein:	29g
Cholesterol:	37mg
Carbohydrates:	81g
Sodium:	1378mg

For **3 servings** each serving contains:

Calories:	414
Fat:	13g
Protein:	19g
Cholesterol:	25mg
Carbohydrates:	54g
Sodium:	919mg

pumpkin-filled shells >>

nutrition info

For **2 servings** each serving contains:

Calories:	910
Fat:	31g
Protein:	47g
Cholesterol:	161mg
Carbohydrates:	116g
Sodium:	802mg

For **3 servings** each serving contains:

Calories:	607
Fat:	21g
Protein:	32g
Cholesterol:	107mg
Carbohydrates:	77g
Sodium:	535mg

I first had pumpkin-filled tortelloni, an unusual delicacy, in the town of Imola near Bologna. This version does not require you to make your own dough and it allows you the benefit of the beta-carotene without the extra work. (KFK)

2 to 3 miniature pumpkins (size of grapefruit, see note)

1 cup nonfat ricotta cheese

1 large egg

¾ teaspoon ground nutmeg

¼ cup pure maple syrup

2 tablespoons minced parsley

6 ounces large dried pasta shells, cooked according to package directions

No-stick cooking spray

sauce

1 cup evaporated 2-percent milk

½ cup freshly grated Parmesan cheese

2 tablespoons sugar

¼ cup crushed pistachio nuts

1 tablespoon cornstarch, mixed with 2 tablespoons cold water

3 tablespoons Madeira

1. Preheat the oven to 400°F.

2. Cook the pumpkins in the microwave on high for 6 minutes. Cut them in half and scoop out the seeds. Remove the pulp and mash the pumpkin—there should be about 2 cups of pulp.

3. Add the cheese, egg, nutmeg, syrup, and parsley. Mix thoroughly. Spoon the filling into the shells and place them in a shallow pan coated with cooking spray.

4. For the sauce, combine all the ingredients in a saucepan and cook over low heat until the sauce is thick, about 5 minutes.

5. Pour the sauce over the shells and bake for 20 minutes.

Note: Do not use jack-o-lantern pumpkins as they are too tough and stringy.

sivanyiyan >>

Sivanyiyan *is a traditional Indian Muslim dish which is served during the Feast of Eid. The noodles, from which the dish gets its name, are very fine wheat-flour noodles. They can be purchased in an Indian market under the name* sivanyiyan, *or at a Middle Eastern grocery under the name* shairyan.

¼ cup corn oil

2 whole cardamom pods

6 ounces dried sivanyiyan or shairyan

2 cups 2-percent milk

2 tablespoons sugar

1. In a skillet, heat the oil over medium heat. Add the cardamom and noodles. Cook, stirring constantly, to brown the noodles without burning them, for about 5 minutes.

2. Add the milk and bring to a boil. Immediately reduce the heat to low. Allow the noodles to absorb the milk until softened, about 10 to 15 minutes. Stir to prevent scorching.

3. Add sugar to taste and cool in the refrigerator. Serve chilled.

evergreen pasta >>

*This medley of vegetables is a culinary study in shades of
green and provides a meal rich in calcium, folic acid, and
isothiocyanates.*

2 cups broccoli florets

1½ cups sliced zucchini (¼-inch-thick slices)

No-stick cooking spray

½ tablespoon unsalted butter

½ cup chopped onion

1 garlic clove, peeled and minced

1 green bell pepper, cut into strips

1 cup sliced mushrooms

Pinch salt

Pinch freshly ground black pepper

6 ounces dried spinach fettucine, cooked
    according to package directions

1 cup chopped tomato

2 tablespoons chopped fresh parsley

¾ cup evaporated skim milk

3 tablespoons freshly grated Parmesan cheese

Freshly ground black pepper to taste

nutrition info

*For **2 servings** each serving
contains:*

Calories:	336
Fat:	8g
Protein:	20g
Cholesterol:	47mg
Carbohydrates:	50g
Sodium:	347mg

*For **3 servings** each serving
contains:*

Calories:	224
Fat:	5g
Protein:	14g
Cholesterol:	31mg
Carbohydrates:	33g
Sodium:	232mg

1. Steam broccoli and zucchini for about 6 minutes. Remove from heat and
rinse lightly with cool water.

2. Meanwhile, spray nonstick skillet with cooking spray. Add the butter
and melt over medium-high heat. Add the onion and garlic and cook,
stirring, until soft, about 2 minutes. Add the green pepper, mushrooms,
salt, and pepper to taste. Cook and stir 1 minute longer.

3. Add the cooked pasta to the vegetable mixture and heat thoroughly. Add
the broccoli and zucchini, tomato, parsley, and milk. Mix well and heat
thoroughly.

4. Serve sprinkled with Parmesan cheese and freshly ground black pepper
to taste.

spaghetti pie >>

The spaghetti forms a lattice design and supports the vegetables and cheese in this truly American dish. The numerous vegetables provide a wide range of phytochemicals for a carbohydrate-loaded meal.

For **2 servings** each serving contains:

Calories:	799
Fat:	22g
Protein:	47g
Cholesterol:	124mg
Carbohydrates:	106g
Sodium:	1659mg

For **3 servings** each serving contains:

Calories:	532
Fat:	15g
Protein:	31g
Cholesterol:	83mg
Carbohydrates:	71g
Sodium:	1106mg

No-stick cooking spray

6 ounces dried spaghetti, cooked according to package directions

1 large egg, beaten

⅓ cup plus 1 tablespoon freshly grated Parmesan cheese

1 tablespoon extra virgin olive oil

1 onion, peeled and chopped

1 garlic clove, peeled and minced

1 small eggplant, diced

1 tomato, diced

1 tablespoon minced fresh basil

¼ cup sliced mushrooms

8 ounces tomato sauce

1 cup low-fat cottage cheese

⅓ cup shredded low-fat mozzarella cheese

1. Preheat the oven to 425°F. Spray a 9-inch pie tin with the cooking spray. Combine the spaghetti, egg, and ⅓ cup Parmesan cheese and press into the pie tin, leaving a well in the center.

2. In a large skillet, heat the oil over medium heat. Add the onion and garlic and cook, stirring, until the onion turns translucent, about 4 to 5 minutes.

3. Add the eggplant, tomato, basil, and mushrooms to the skillet and continue to cook, stirring, for 5 minutes. Add the tomato sauce and cook until the vegetables are tender, about 10 minutes.

4. Spoon the vegetables and sauce into the center of the pie tin. Spoon the cottage cheese around the edges of the sauce. Top the vegetables with the remaining Parmesan and the mozzarella and bake for 30 minutes or until the cheese is melted and bubbly and the spaghetti crust begins to brown.

tortelli di spinaci >>

We have gone neoclassical redefining this traditional Italian dish with a small amount of chili paste. This recipe takes a little more work since you are making homemade pasta. It is well worth the effort.

1 teaspoon extra virgin olive oil

1 garlic clove, peeled and minced

1 small onion, peeled and diced

8 ounces fresh spinach, rinsed and trimmed

8 ounces nonfat ricotta cheese

1½ teaspoons freshly grated Parmesan cheese

Salt and freshly ground black pepper to taste

1 cup unbleached all-purpose flour

2 large eggs

1 egg white

¼ teaspoon salt

sauce

1 tablespoon extra virgin olive oil

1 garlic clove, peeled and minced

1 tablespoon chopped fresh basil

2 cups pureed tomatoes

¼ cup burgundy wine

3 tablespoons chopped fresh parsley

1 teaspoon chili paste

1. In a skillet, heat the oil over medium heat. Add the garlic and onion to the skillet and cook, stirring, for 2 minutes. Add the spinach and cook until wilted. Drain well and puree in a food processor. Add the cheeses and salt and pepper to taste.

2. Place the flour in a large bowl, forming a well in the center. Add 1 whole egg and 1 egg white to the well. Add the salt.

3. Slowly work the flour into the well with a fork until a soft ball forms. Knead for 10 minutes or until smooth.

4. Roll out the dough to ⅛ inch thickness. Cut the dough into 2-inch squares and brush them with 1 beaten egg. Place 1 teaspoon of the spinach and cheese mixture into the center of each square. Fold each one in half to form a triangle and pinch the sides closed to seal in the filling. Alternatively, use a ravioli plaque.

5. Boil the tortelli in lightly salted water for 3 to 5 minutes until tender.

6. In a large skillet, heat the olive oil over medium heat. Add the garlic and basil, and cook, stirring, for 1 minute. Reduce the heat to low, add the tomatoes and wine, and cook for 30 minutes to reduce the sauce. Add the parsley and chili paste and cook for 5 minutes. Serve over the spinach tortelli.

Note: If you don't have time to make your own dough, substitute wonton skins.

To avoid breaking the tortelli, remove them from the boiling water with a slotted spoon.

A ravioli plaque is a small tray that assists with ravioli preparation. They are available at kitchen stores.

vegetable lasagna >>

nutrition info

For **2 servings** each serving contains:

Calories:	828
Fat:	30g
Protein:	66g
Cholesterol:	85mg
Carbohydrates:	82g
Sodium:	2149mg

For **3 servings** each serving contains:

Calories:	552
Fat:	20g
Protein:	44g
Cholesterol:	57mg
Carbohydrates:	54g
Sodium:	1433mg

For high-test fuel, we have whole-wheat pasta.

5 whole-wheat lasagna noodles, cooked according to package directions

8 ounces fresh spinach, washed

½ tablespoon extra virgin olive oil

1 cup sliced mushrooms

1 cup sliced carrots (2 medium carrots)

⅓ cup chopped onion

8 ounces canned tomato sauce

3 ounces salt-free tomato paste

¾ teaspoon dried oregano

1½ teaspoons chopped fresh basil

No-stick cooking spray

1 cup 1-percent fat cottage cheese

8 ounces part-skim milk mozzarella cheese, shredded

6 tablespoons freshly grated Parmesan cheese

1 sweet yellow bell pepper, sliced into rings

1. Preheat the oven to 375°F.

2. Rinse the lasagna noodles well and drain. Rinse the spinach and place in covered saucepan; do not add water (the water drops left on the spinach leaves are enough). Cook over medium-high heat. When steam forms, reduce heat to low and cook until spinach wilts, about 3 to 5 minutes. Remove from heat.

3. In nonstick skillet, heat the oil over medium heat. Add the mushrooms, carrots, and onion and cook, stirring, until tender, about 5 minutes. Stir in the tomato sauce, tomato paste, oregano, and basil.

4. Lightly spray an 8 × 8 × 2-inch pan with cooking spray and layer the noodles, cottage cheese, spinach, mozzarella, tomato sauce, and Parmesan cheese in the pan. Repeat layers, ending with Parmesan cheese. Top with yellow bell pepper rings. Bake 50 minutes, or until top begins to brown lightly. Let stand 10 minutes before serving.

panulla >>

All the glory that is Rome is contained in this aromatic blend of fresh vegetables. We must confess, this recipe was brought directly from Italy by a close friend. We're sure that you'll enjoy it as much as we do.

2 tablespoons plus 1 teaspoon extra virgin olive oil

3 garlic cloves, minced

2 pepperoncini, seeded and diced

3 tablespoons minced fresh parsley

1 head radicchio, quartered

8 ounces dried pasta of your choice, cooked according to package directions

5 ounces asparagus, cut into 1-inch pieces and steamed

5 ounces green beans, cut into 1-inch pieces and steamed

1. In a large skillet heat the 2 tablespoons oil over high heat. Add the garlic, pepperoncini, and parsley and cook, stirring, for 5 minutes.

2. Meanwhile, sprinkle the radicchio with the remaining oil. Grill or broil for 5 minutes.

3. Pour the drained pasta into the garlic and parsley sauce. Toss to coat.

4. Add the asparagus, green beans, and raddichio and serve.

*tantalizing
tubers
and really
good roots*

baked onion rings >>

Although not especially aesthetic, these tasty onion rings make a great topping or side dish for a veggie burger.

1 large sweet onion, peeled and thickly sliced crosswise

½ cup plain nonfat yogurt

¼ teaspoon salt

2 garlic cloves, peeled and minced

1½ tablespoons sesame seeds, toasted (page 112)

Paprika

1. Preheat the oven to 375°F.

2. Place separated onion rings on a nonstick cookie sheet. In a bowl, combine the yogurt, salt, and garlic. Brush or spoon the mixture onto the onion rings. Sprinkle with sesame seeds and paprika. Bake for 25 minutes, or until brown.

carrot blinis >>

For a sweet dose of beta-carotene, try these delicious little Russian-style pancakes.

4 medium carrots, scraped and shredded

2 tablespoons dehydrated minced onion

2 large eggs

2 tablespoons wheat germ

2 tablespoons bread crumbs

½ teaspoon salt

⅛ teaspoon freshly ground black pepper

No-stick cooking spray

Nonfat or low-fat sour cream or Yogurt Cheese (page 68) (optional)

1. Combine all ingredients except cooking spray and sour cream in a food processor and coarsely chop. Spray a nonstick griddle or skillet with cooking spray and heat over medium-high heat.

2. Spoon 1 heaping tablespoon of batter for each pancake onto the griddle or skillet and flatten slightly. Flip the pancakes over to cook the other side when the edges begin to brown. Cook the pancakes until they are brown on both sides. Serve with a dollop of nonfat or low-fat sour cream, if desired.

nutrition info

For **2 servings** each serving contains:

Calories:	186
Fat:	6g
Protein:	10g
Cholesterol:	187mg
Carbohydrates:	26g
Sodium:	694mg

For **3 servings** each serving contains:

Calories:	124
Fat:	4g
Protein:	6g
Cholesterol:	125mg
Carbohydrates:	17g
Sodium:	463mg

jerusalem artichokes and lentils >>

nutrition info

For 2 servings each serving contains:

Calories:	408
Fat:	3g
Protein:	22g
Cholesterol:	0mg
Carbohydrates:	76g
Sodium:	553mg

For 3 servings each serving contains:

Calories:	272
Fat:	2g
Protein:	15g
Cholesterol:	0mg
Carbohydrates:	51g
Sodium:	369mg

Jerusalem artichokes have a much lighter taste than potatoes and lend a delicious flavor to this hearty dish.

½ cup plus 2 tablespoons red lentils

½ cup plus 2 tablespoons water

1 small bay leaf

1 garlic clove, peeled and minced

1 teaspoon vegetable oil

½ teaspoon salt

6 Jerusalem artichokes, quartered

2 tablespoons chopped green pepper

2 tablespoons chopped pimento

½ tablespoon paprika

1. In a saucepan, cover the lentils with water. Add the bay leaf, garlic, oil, and salt. Bring to a boil over high heat. Reduce heat to low, cover, and cook until the lentils are tender but still hold their shape, about 15 to 20 minutes. Drain remaining liquid. Remove the bay leaf.

2. Meanwhile, steam the Jerusalem artichokes until tender, 12 to 15 minutes. Add the artichokes, green pepper, pimento, and paprika to the lentils. Cover and place over low heat for 5 minutes or so, until flavors mellow together. Serve.

mustard seed potatoes >>

This fragrant Castillian dish is most often found at tapas bars. The different mustard seeds are available at supermarkets with good gourmet sections or at gourmet food stores.

½ **pound small red skin potatoes**

⅔ **tablespoon extra virgin olive oil**

½ **teaspoon black mustard seeds**

½ **teaspoon yellow mustard seeds**

½ **teaspoon cumin seed**

½ **teaspoon salt**

¼ **teaspoon freshly ground black pepper**

1. Preheat the oven to 375°F. Lightly coat the potatoes with the olive oil.

2. Place all the spices into a plastic bag and mix together. Place the potatoes in the bag, seal the bag, and shake to coat the potatoes with the seasonings.

3. Place the potatoes on a pan and bake for 30 minutes or until tender.

nutrition info

For **2 servings** each serving contains:

Calories:	140
Fat:	5g
Protein:	3g
Cholesterol:	0mg
Carbohydrates:	21g
Sodium:	541mg

For **3 servings** each serving contains:

Calories:	93
Fat:	3g
Protein:	2g
Cholesterol:	0mg
Carbohydrates:	14g
Sodium:	361mg

potato masala >>

This classic Indian dish is often served with indigenous flat bread. For an easy substitute, use pita bread.

nutrition info

For **2 servings** each serving contains:

Calories:	364
Fat:	8g
Protein:	7g
Cholesterol:	0mg
Carbohydrates:	65g
Sodium:	24mg

For **3 servings** each serving contains:

Calories:	242
Fat:	5g
Protein:	5g
Cholesterol:	0mg
Carbohydrates:	43g
Sodium:	16mg

1 tablespoon safflower oil

½ teaspoon black mustard seeds

2 medium onions, peeled and thinly sliced

2 garlic cloves, peeled and chopped

One 1-inch piece fresh ginger, peeled and minced

2 jalapeño chilies, quartered

¼ teaspoon turmeric

½ cup chopped cilantro

1 tablespoon fresh lemon juice

Salt to taste

2 tablespoons water

4 potatoes, cooked, peeled, and mashed

1. In a large skillet heat the oil over high heat and add the mustard seeds. When they begin to sputter, add the onions and cook, stirring, until transluscent.

2. Add the garlic, ginger, chilies, and turmeric, and cook, stirring, 2 minutes.

3. Add the cilantro, lemon juice, salt, and water. When the water boils, add the potatoes. Mix well and serve.

root vegetable melange >>

Melanges are mixtures quite common in France. And if you've never known what to do with rutabaga, parsnips, and turnips, here's a sweet first recipe to try.

1½ cups vegetable broth (page 71)

1 cup peeled and diced rutabaga

1 cup peeled and diced turnips

1 cup peeled and diced parsnips

1 cup peeled and diced sweet potatoes

1 small onion, coarsely chopped

2 carrots, coarsely chopped

One 6-ounce can frozen orange juice concentrate

½ cup brown sugar

¼ cup brandy (optional)

1 tablespoon cornstarch, mixed with 2 tablespoons cold water

One 11-ounce can mandarin oranges, drained

nutrition info

*For **2 servings** each serving contains:*

Calories:	676
Fat:	2g
Protein:	8g
Cholesterol:	0mg
Carbohydrates:	147g
Sodium:	577mg

*For **3 servings** each serving contains:*

Calories:	451
Fat:	1g
Protein:	5g
Cholesterol:	0mg
Carbohydrates:	98g
Sodium:	384mg

1. Preheat the oven to 350°F.

2. In a large saucepan, bring the vegetable broth to a boil. Add the rutabaga and turnips and cook for 5 minutes. Add the parsnips and sweet potatoes. Continue cooking for an additional 5 minutes. Remove the vegetables with a slotted spoon and reserve the broth. Place the vegetables in an oven-safe, 2-quart casserole dish. Mix in the onion and carrots.

3. In a smaller saucepan, combine the orange juice concentrate, sugar, broth, and brandy. Mix thoroughly. Stir in the cornstarch mixture and heat over medium heat until sauce begins to thicken. Add the oranges and simmer for 5 minutes.

4. Pour the orange sauce over the vegetables. Bake for 30 minutes or until tender.

spicy caramelized parsnips >>

Parsnips are usually sweet and cook up wonderfully tender. But sometimes they can be bitter and woody. Ask your grocer about the quality of the parsnips before you purchase them.

1 teaspoon unsalted butter

1 small onion, peeled and sliced

4 ounces parsnips, peeled and sliced (about 2 medium parsnips)

1 teaspoon paprika

1½ tablespoons crystallized ginger, chopped

1 cup water

1. In a nonstick skillet, melt the butter over low heat. Add the onion and parsnips and cook, stirring, for about 12 minutes. Add the paprika and ginger and continue to cook another 5 to 7 minutes, or until the vegetables are caramelized.

2. Add the water and cover, cooking until the water evaporates and the parsnips are tender, about 20 minutes. Serve.

sweet potato
casserole >>

While working with cardiology patients at Duke University's Preventive Approach to Cardiology program, I had to design a recipe that Southern sweet-potato lovers would enjoy, but without all of the fat. This was the successful outcome. (SMK)

2 medium sweet potatoes

½ tablespoon unsalted butter

½ cup crushed pineapple

2 tablespoons chopped walnuts

⅛ teaspoon nutmeg

No-stick cooking spray

1. Cook whole potatoes in a large pot of boiling water for 25 minutes or until tender. Peel and mash. Stir in the butter, pineapple, walnuts, and nutmeg and mix thoroughly.

2. Preheat the oven to 375°F. Spray a 1-quart casserole and add the potato mixture. Bake uncovered for 25 minutes.

Note: To save time, potatoes can be cooked in the microwave, but they will not be quite as fluffy.

nutrition info

*For **2 servings** each serving contains:*

Calories:	256
Fat:	8g
Protein:	5g
Cholesterol:	8mg
Carbohydrates:	44g
Sodium:	21mg

*For **3 servings** each serving contains:*

Calories:	171
Fat:	5g
Protein:	3g
Cholesterol:	5mg
Carbohydrates:	29g
Sodium:	14mg

swiss chard
torta >>

This layered casserole is a wonderful source of phytoestrogens and antioxidants.

1 tablespoon fresh lemon juice

¼ cup water

12 leaves Swiss chard

3 medium potatoes, thinly sliced

2 large eggs, beaten

8 ounces nonfat soy sausage, cooked and crumbled

Salt and freshly ground black pepper to taste

1. Place the lemon juice and water in a microwave-safe dish with a lid. Add the Swiss chard and steam, covered, in the microwave oven on high for 3 minutes or until the chard wilts.

2. Coat the potatoes with the beaten eggs. Layer a baking dish with 1 layer of Swiss chard, followed by the potatoes and sausage. Add a sprinkle of salt and pepper.

3. Continue layering until all the ingredients are used up. The top layer can be either sausage or potato, but not Swiss chard.

4. Bake for 30 to 40 minutes at 375°F or until the potatoes are tender.

yam tzimmes >>

Tzimmes is the Eastern European version of the French melange. In this recipe, we've removed the traditional high-fat brisket and created a sweeter version using yams and dried fruits in place of potatoes and carrots. Now it's the ideal high-performance vegetarian dish.

2 medium yams, peeled and cubed

¼ cup golden raisins

8 pitted prunes, coarsely chopped

¼ cup chopped walnuts

¼ cup pure maple syrup

1. Preheat the oven to 375°F.

2. Combine all ingredients in a casserole and bake covered for 30 minutes, or until the yams are soft. Mix to blend flavors before serving.

nutrition info

For **2 servings** each serving contains:

Calories:	634
Fat:	10g
Protein:	10g
Cholesterol:	0mg
Carbohydrates:	135g
Sodium:	36mg

For **3 servings** each serving contains:

Calories:	423
Fat:	6g
Protein:	7g
Cholesterol:	0mg
Carbohydrates:	90g
Sodium:	24mg

CHAPTER TEN >>>

vivacious
vegetables

hearty artichoke
pie >>

The heart of this dish is the low-fat cheese sauce. I use this dish for entertaining as an appetizer or as part of a buffet offering. It is always high on the list of recipe requests. (KFK)

One 14 ounce-can artichoke hearts, drained and chopped

¼ cup low-fat mayonnaise

¼ cup Yogurt Cheese (page 68)

½ cup freshly grated Parmesan cheese

2 tablespoons canned or cooked red chilies

½ teaspoon yellow mustard

½ teaspoon chopped garlic

1 package refrigerator bread dough (Pillsbury Crusty French Bread)

1. Preheat the oven to 350°F.

2. In a large bowl, combine all the ingredients (except bread dough) and mix well.

3. Open the dough and unroll flat at the seam. Place the dough in a 9-inch pie pan with all excess dough hanging off one side of the pan. Trim the dough reserving the large square for the top crust.

4. Place the artichoke mixture onto the dough and cover with the second piece of dough. Trim excess and crimp sides. Poke some holes in the top of the pie with a fork to vent pie.

5. Bake for 30 to 40 minutes or until lightly browned.

confetti coleslaw >>

As you celebrate your winning time, your oxygen consumption may have hit an all-time high. This side dish filled with antioxidants is an essential component of your victory meal.

¼ cup low-fat mayonnaise

¼ cup plain nonfat yogurt

1½ tablespoons fresh lemon juice

1½ tablespoons sugar

1½ tablespoons herb seasoning mix

3 cups shredded red and/or green cabbage

½ cup shredded carrots

In a large bowl, combine all the ingredients and serve.

nutrition info

*For **2 servings** each serving contains:*

Calories:	168
Fat:	6g
Protein:	4g
Cholesterol:	8mg
Carbohydrates:	27g
Sodium:	204mg

*For **3 servings** each serving contains:*

Calories:	112
Fat:	4g
Protein:	2g
Cholesterol:	5mg
Carbohydrates:	18g
Sodium:	136mg

broccoli lentil
salad >>

After a hard run, this chilled, aromatic salad can be a refreshing addition to your meal. Cottage cheese never tasted so good.

½ cup 1-percent low-fat cottage cheese

½ teaspoon fresh lemon juice

¼ cup lowfat buttermilk

1 medium carrot, scraped and finely grated

1 tablespoon grated onion

1 teaspoon lemon peel

¼ teaspoon dried dill

⅛ teaspoon dried thyme

⅛ teaspoon dried basil

⅛ teaspoon dried oregano

⅛ teaspoon dried marjoram

¼ teaspoon freshly ground black pepper

½ cup lentils

1½ cups water

1 teaspoon salt

½ cup chopped celery

¼ cup chopped scallions

2 cups chopped broccoli

Salt and freshly ground black pepper to taste

1. In a blender or small food processor, combine the cottage cheese, lemon juice, and buttermilk. Process at low speed until smooth. Place in a mixing bowl and add the carrot, onion, lemon peel, dill, thyme, basil, oregano, marjoram, and ⅛ teaspoon black pepper. Mix thoroughly.

2. Place the lentils and water in a large saucepan and bring to a boil over high heat. Cover, reduce heat to low, and cook for 20 minutes, or until the lentils are tender but still hold their shape. Drain and add the salt, ⅛ teaspoon pepper, and buttermilk dressing mixture. Chill in the refrigerator, and when it is cold, add the celery, scallions, and broccoli. Season with salt and pepper.

eggplant with artichoke sauce, keka style >>

*For **2 servings** each serving contains:*

Calories:	439
Fat:	13g
Protein:	41g
Cholesterol:	30mg
Carbohydrates:	44g
Sodium:	829mg

*For **3 servings** each serving contains:*

Calories:	293
Fat:	9g
Protein:	28g
Cholesterol:	20mg
Carbohydrates:	29g
Sodium:	553mg

The seitan in this recipe is a real protein booster. One serving of this dish and you'll probably have met over half of your day's protein needs.

artichoke sauce

2 teaspoons extra virgin olive oil

2 tomatoes, diced

½ onion, minced

¼ teaspoon dried oregano

1 garlic clove, peeled and minced

1 artichoke heart, chopped

½ cup tomato juice

Salt and freshly ground black pepper to taste

eggplant tubes

Olive oil cooking spray

2 miniature eggplants, sliced ¼ inch thick lengthwise

1 leek, white part only

3 ounces low-fat gouda cheese, cut into ½ × 1-inch strips

6 ounces seitan, premarinated, shredded

1. Preheat the oven to 375°F.

2. For the sauce, heat the olive oil in a saucepan over high heat, and cook the tomatoes, onion, oregano, and garlic, stirring, until the onion becomes transluscent and the tomatoes begin to soften, about 7 minutes.

3. Add the artichoke, tomato juice, and salt and pepper. Simmer for 3 minutes. Puree in a blender until smooth.

4. Prepare a grill. Lightly spray the olive oil cooking spray on the eggplants and leek. Grill for 3 minutes on each side.

5. Place each slice of eggplant flat. Add a piece of leek, a strip of cheese, and some seitan. Roll into a tube and place in a baking dish. Continue until all the eggplant is used up.

6. Pour the sauce over the eggplant tubes and bake for 10 minutes or until all the ingredients are warmed. Serve with the sauce.

gingered
asparagus >>

nutrition info

For **2 servings** each serving contains:

Calories:	112
Fat:	4g
Protein:	6g
Cholesterol:	0mg
Carbohydrates:	16g
Sodium:	270mg

For **3 servings** each serving contains:

Calories:	74
Fat:	3g
Protein:	4g
Cholesterol:	0mg
Carbohydrates:	11g
Sodium:	180mg

The use of ginger in Asian herbal medicine is well documented. But just as important, we like what ginger adds to the taste of asparagus.

1½ teaspoons peanut oil

1 pound fresh asparagus, trimmed

1 medium carrot, scraped and shredded

⅓ cup shredded red bell pepper

1½ tablespoons finely shredded fresh ginger

1 tablespoon low-sodium soy sauce

Dash white pepper

Few drops sesame oil

1. In a nonstick skillet, heat the oil over medium heat. Add the asparagus and cook, stirring, for 30 seconds. Add the carrot, red pepper, and ginger, and cook, stirring, for another 15 seconds. Add the soy sauce and white pepper and stir-fry until the vegetables are slightly softened but still crisp, about 3 minutes.

2. Remove from the heat and sprinkle lightly with sesame oil. Serve.

grilled brussels sprouts >>

Brussels sprouts are so healthful yet are often an acquired taste. This marinade makes acquiring it a delight.

15 Brussels sprouts

1½ tablespoons Dijon mustard

1½ tablespoons coarse-grain mustard

1½ tablespoons rice vinegar

½ tablespoon extra virgin olive oil

1½ tablespoons apple cider

1 scallion, minced

½ tablespoon chopped fresh sage (or ½ teaspoon dried sage)

⅛ teaspoon freshly ground black pepper

1. Trim the bases and remove any yellowed outside leaves of the sprouts. Slice the sprouts in half lengthwise unless they are very small.

2. In a bowl, combine the remaining ingredients. Add the Brussels sprouts and marinate for 30 minutes at room temperature or for 1 hour in the refrigerator. Skewer the sprouts or place them in a grilling basket or pan and cook over medium-hot coals for 12 to 14 minutes. Remove from the fire and serve.

nutrition info

For *2 servings* each serving contains:

Calories:	128
Fat:	5g
Protein:	7g
Cholesterol:	0mg
Carbohydrates:	19g
Sodium:	329mg

For *3 servings* each serving contains:

Calories:	85
Fat:	3g
Protein:	4g
Cholesterol:	0mg
Carbohydrates:	13g
Sodium:	219mg

grilled eggplant and fennel
sandwich >>

Vegetarian sandwiches have long been a European staple. This is a great sandwich to try with the homemade Focaccia on page 90.

1 small eggplant

Salt

1 fennel bulb

3 tablespoons extra virgin olive oil

3 tablespoons red wine vinegar

2 tablespoons minced fresh basil

½ teaspoon freshly ground black pepper

3 plum tomatoes, sliced

Six ¾-inch-thick slices Italian bread

2 tablespoons slivered fresh basil

1. Prepare eggplant by slicing (unpeeled) into rounds, arrange on paper towel, sprinkle with salt, and allow to drain for 30 minutes. Wipe the salt and moisture off before placing in the marinade.

2. Prepare the fennel by cutting off the stalks even with the top of bulb, trimming the base, and removing the tough outer layers. Slice the bulb vertically into slices ½ inch wide.

3. Combine the oil, vinegar, basil, and pepper and toss in a bowl with the eggplant, fennel, and tomatoes. Marinate at least 20 minutes, turning frequently.

4. Meanwhile, prepare a grill. Place the marinated vegetables in a grilling basket or pan and cook over medium-hot coals for 10 to 12 minutes, turning once halfway through and basting lightly with the marinade.

5. While the vegetables cook, toast the bread slices on both sides until golden alongside the vegetables.

6. To serve, place one slice of bread on each plate, and top it with eggplant, tomatoes, and fennel. Sprinkle with the basil and top with the second slice of bread.

moo shoo vegetables >>

The tofu takes on the wonderful Asian flavors. (The dried mushroom mixture is often found in the produce section of supermarkets or in Asian groceries.)

6 tablespoons low-sodium soy sauce

¼ cup sweet cooking rice wine

½ pound low-fat firm tofu, cut into 1- to 2-inch-long strips, ¼ inch thick

1 ounce dried stir-fry mushroom mixture soaked in 1 cup boiling water or 1¾ ounces fresh tigerlily buds and ½ ounce mo-er mushrooms

1 whole large egg and 1 egg white, well beaten

No-stick cooking spray

2 tablespoons peanut oil

3½ ounces enoki or crimini mushrooms

3 cups shredded Napa cabbage

5 ounces canned sliced bamboo shoots, drained

2 cups mung bean sprouts

½ cup vegetable broth (page 71)

1 teaspoon sesame oil

6 moo shu pancakes (recipe follows)

Cooked rice (optional)

1. In a bowl, combine 4 tablespoons soy sauce and 2 teaspoons cooking wine. Add the tofu and marinate it for about 20 minutes. If using fresh tiger lily buds and mushrooms, cut the buds in half and the mushrooms into small pieces.

2. In a large nonstick skillet or wok over medium heat, quickly scramble and cook the egg and egg white and remove from the skillet. Cut into small pieces and set aside.

3. Using the same skillet, spray it and add the peanut oil. Heat over medium-high heat and add the remaining vegetables, stirring rapidly for about 5 minutes. Remove from the skillet, and add the tofu with marinade, stirring quickly for 1 to 2 minutes. Add the vegetable broth, cover, reduce the heat to medium, and cook for 2 minutes. Add the vegetables, remaining soy sauce, and cooking wine, and stir for about 45 seconds. Add the eggs and sesame oil, stirring rapidly for 20 seconds. Serve in warmed moo shu pancakes or over rice.

moo shoo pancakes

These can be purchased at Asian grocery stores or you may use the following recipe.

½ cup all-purpose flour

Dash salt

2 large eggs, beaten

½ cup skim milk

1½ teaspoons unsalted butter, melted

No-stick cooking spray

1. In a bowl, combine the flour, salt, eggs, milk, and butter. Mix thoroughly and allow to sit for 20 minutes.

2. Heat a nonstick skillet over high heat for 30 seconds, and then spray it with cooking spray. Mix the batter and spoon 2½ to 3 tablespoons into the skillet to form a thin layer. Cook until firm, about 3 minutes, and then turn the pancake over and cook the other side about 10 seconds. Remove from the skillet and repeat until you make 6 pancakes. Stir the batter each time before use.

rainbow cheese
soufflé >>

The pot at the end of this rainbow is filled with phytochemicals, antioxidants, and calcium.

Vegetable cooking spray

1½ cups cauliflower florets

1½ cups broccoli florets

1 cup low-sodium vegetable broth (page 71)

¼ cup crumbled feta cheese

4 tablespoons unbleached all-purpose flour

1 tablespoon unsalted butter, melted

2 teaspoons fresh oregano (or 1 teaspoon dried)

½ teaspoon fresh thyme (or ¼ teaspoon dried)

½ teaspoon salt

¼ teaspoon white pepper

4 egg whites, whipped to soft-peak stage

1 yellow bell pepper, cored and diced

1 red bell pepper, cored and diced

1. Preheat the oven to 350°F. Lightly spray a 6-cup soufflé pan and set aside.

2. Place the cauliflower and broccoli in a microwave-safe bowl with the broth. Cook in the microwave oven on high for 10 minutes.

3. Drain the vegetables and separate the broccoli and cauliflower. Place the cauliflower in a food processor and process until smooth. Add half the feta cheese, flour, butter, fresh oregano, fresh thyme, salt, and pepper. Process until smooth. Slowly fold half the egg whites into the cauliflower and place the mixture in a 6-cup soufflé pan. Sprinkle with the red bell pepper.

4. Put the broccoli in a food processor and process to smooth. Add remaining feta cheese, butter, oregano, thyme, flour, salt, and pepper. Process until smooth. Slowly fold the remaining egg whites into the broccoli and pour on top of the cauliflower mixture. Sprinkle with the yellow bell pepper.

5. Bake for 50 minutes or until golden and puffy.

new mexico
tacos >>

We stuff our tacos with antioxidants.

1 tablespoon canola oil

1 cup broccoli florets

½ cup mushrooms, sliced

½ cup red pepper, diced

3 scallions, diced

3 or 4 large flour tortillas (made without lard)

3 ounces grated low-fat cheddar cheese

¼ cup salsa

¼ cup Yogurt Cheese (page 68)

¼ cup julienned jicama

1. In a large skillet, heat the oil over medium heat. Add the broccoli, mushrooms, pepper, and scallions and cook, stirring, for 2 to 3 minutes. Place ¼ to ⅓ of the mixture in the center of tortilla.

2. Sprinkle with cheddar cheese and fold the tortilla in half. Bake for 5 minutes at 400°F or until the cheese melts.

3. Spoon the salsa and Yogurt Cheese on top of the taco. Sprinkle with the jicama and enjoy.

spaghetti squash >>

This dish would be great made with pasta, but it wouldn't have the delightful crunch that spaghetti squash offers.

One 8-inch spaghetti squash (about ½ pound), sliced in half lengthwise

No-stick cooking spray

2 shallots, peeled and chopped

1 large garlic clove, crushed

⅛ teaspoon freshly ground black pepper

2 tablespoons freshly chopped chives

3 fresh tomatoes, chopped

1. Preheat the oven to 375°F.

2. Scoop out the seeds and place the squash cut side down in a microwave-safe dish. Fill the dish with ¼-inch water, and cover with microwave-safe plastic wrap, leaving one corner unsealed. Cook in the microwave oven on high for 15 minutes or until the squash is tender and easily pierced by a fork. Let cool.

3. Meanwhile, spray a nonstick skillet with cooking spray and heat it over medium heat. Sauté the shallots, garlic, pepper, and chives, stirring, until the shallots are transluscent, 3 to 5 minutes. Add the tomatoes and cook until most of the liquid is gone, about 2 to 3 minutes.

4. Scoop out the squash, using a fork to make the strands. Toss the strands with the sauteed mixture and serve.

nutrition info

For **2 servings** each serving contains:

Calories:	111
Fat:	<1g
Protein:	4g
Cholesterol:	0mg
Carbohydrates:	25g
Sodium:	42mg

For **3 servings** each serving contains:

Calories:	74
Fat:	<1g
Protein:	3g
Cholesterol:	0mg
Carbohydrates:	17g
Sodium:	28mg

195

spinach-stuffed
succhini >>

nutrition info

*For **2 servings** each serving contains:*

Calories:	1153
Fat:	20g
Protein:	49g
Cholesterol:	44mg
Carbohydrates:	203g
Sodium:	855mg

*For **3 servings** each serving contains:*

Calories:	769
Fat:	13g
Protein:	33g
Cholesterol:	29mg
Carbohydrates:	136g
Sodium:	570mg

Pardon our spelling, but we must Say that this Scrumptious, Savory Selection is Sensational!

1¾ cups (14 ounces) low-sodium vegetable broth (page 71)

2 cups instant brown rice

8 ounces fresh spinach, washed and chopped

One 28-ounce can low-sodium crushed tomatoes

2 teaspoons garlic powder

1 teaspoon fresh basil

1 teaspoon fresh oregano

¼ cup freshly grated Parmesan cheese

½ cup fat-free ricotta cheese

Four 6-inch-long zucchini

½ cup shredded low-fat mozzarella

1. Bring the vegetable broth to a boil over high heat in a large saucepan. Add the rice and spinach. Reduce the heat to low, cover, and cook until the broth is absorbed, about 10 minutes.

2. Add the tomatoes, garlic powder, basil, oregano, Parmesan, and ricotta to the rice and mix thoroughly. Cook for 5 minutes.

3. Slice the zucchini in half lengthwise. With a spoon, scrape out the seeds to form a cavity.

4. Spoon the rice into the cavity and place the zucchini in a baking dish. Sprinkle with mozzarella cheese. Broil for 5 minutes or until cheese is melted.

squash patties >>

You don't have to squash these patties to make them.

½ **pound green summer squash**

½ **pound yellow summer squash**

2 **tablespoons unflavored bread crumbs**

1 **large egg, beaten**

½ **cup pot cheese, mashed**

1 **tablespoon unsalted butter, melted**

No-stick cooking spray

1. Preheat the oven to 350°F.

2. Peel and grate the squash. In a large bowl, combine the grated squash and bread crumbs and toss until the squash is coated.

3. In a bowl, blend the egg, cheese, and butter until smooth and combine with the squash until well blended.

4. Coat a nonstick cookie sheet with the cooking spray. Place 3-inch circles of the squash mixture onto the cookie sheet.

5. Bake for 20 minutes.

nutrition info

For 2 servings each serving contains:

Calories:	310
Fat:	21g
Protein:	16g
Cholesterol:	160mg
Carbohydrates:	15g
Sodium:	437mg

For 3 servings each serving contains:

Calories:	207
Fat:	14g
Protein:	11g
Cholesterol:	107mg
Carbohydrates:	10g
Sodium:	291mg

stuffed savoy >>

Savoy cabbage is a member of the Brassica *family, rich in isothiocyanates.*

1½ teaspoons canola oil

½ red bell pepper, minced

½ green bell pepper, minced

1 small eggplant, peeled and diced

½ medium tomato, diced

1½ teaspoons minced garlic

4 sun-dried tomatoes, minced

4 ounces quick-cooking couscous (about 1 cup)

⅓ cup salted water

¼ teaspoon saffron

4 large or 6 small savoy cabbage leaves, wilted

½ cup tomato sauce, heated

1. In a large skillet, heat the oil over high heat. Add the red pepper, green pepper, eggplant, tomato, garlic, and sun-dried tomatoes and cook, stirring, for 5 minutes. Cover and allow the vegetables to cook for 10 minutes. Reduce the heat to low and cook for 15 minutes more.

2. Meanwhile, in a saucepan cook the couscous in the salted water with the saffron. Pour the vegetables onto the cooked couscous after it has absorbed all the water and mix thoroughly.

3. Place a portion of the couscous mixture at the end of each cabbage leaf and roll. Serve with the tomato sauce.

vegetable
bulgur >>

We have traveled to Kurdistan for this flavorful traditional staple. Bulgur wheat is an excellent source of nutrients and a great carbohydrate load for weekend warriors.

1 teaspoon canola oil

1 small onion, peeled and chopped

½ cup chopped okra

1 small tomato, finely chopped

2 cups water

1 cup bulgur

1½ teaspoons crystallized ginger

1 teaspoon ground coriander

1. In a skillet over medium heat, heat the oil and cook the onion and okra for 2 to 3 minutes.

2. Add the tomato and water and bring to a boil. Add the bulgur, ginger, and coriander. Reduce the heat to low and simmer for 20 minutes, stirring occasionally.

nutrition info

For **2 servings** *each serving contains:*

Calories:	295
Fat:	4g
Protein:	10g
Cholesterol:	0mg
Carbohydrates:	61g
Sodium:	26mg

For **3 servings** *each serving contains:*

Calories:	197
Fat:	2g
Protein:	7g
Cholesterol:	0mg
Carbohydrates:	41g
Sodium:	18mg

szechuan stuffed
red peppers >>

Our version of the Eastern European stuffed pepper owes more to the Szechuan region of China than to Budapest. While Szechuan cooking is usually assumed to be hot, this mild sauce complements the stuffed peppers to perfection.

szechuan sauce

2 tablespoons tamari sauce or regular soy sauce

2 tablespoons rice vinegar

2 tablespoons apple cider

1 tablespoon honey

1 tablespoon plum sauce

1 tablespoon tomato paste

1 teaspoon Dijon mustard

stuffed red peppers

1 cup raw long-grain brown or white rice

No-stick cooking spray

1 tablespoon peanut oil

2 tablespoons finely chopped celery

2 tablespoons finely chopped green bell pepper

2 tablespoons finely chopped red bell pepper

2 tablespoons finely chopped onion

6 ounces firm tofu, crumbled

2 large or 3 small red bell peppers, stem and seeds removed

4 medium tomatoes, quartered

1. To make the sauce, combine all the ingredients in a bowl and mix well. Set aside.

2. Cook rice using ½ cup less water than recommended on the package, until the water is absorbed and the rice is almost tender.

3. Spray a nonstick skillet and add the oil. Heat over medium-high heat and add the chopped vegetables. Cook, stirring, until almost tender, about 5 minutes. Remove from the heat and add the rice, tofu, and ¼ cup of Szechuan sauce. Mix well.

4. Slightly trim the bottoms of the peppers so that they can stand upright. Stuff the filling into the peppers, and stand the peppers upright in one layer in a heavy-bottomed saucepan. Push the tomatoes all around the peppers, squeezing the tomatoes slightly to release some juice.

5. Bring the tomato juice on the peppers to a boil over medium heat, cover tightly, reduce heat to medium-low, and cook for about 30 minutes or until the peppers are tender.

6. Remove the peppers to a serving dish and keep warm. Puree half of the pan juices and 2 tablespoons of the Szechuan sauce in a blender. Pour the pureed mixture over and around the peppers and serve immediately.

watercress tortilla >>

Few people know what to do with watercress. Here we've created a cosmopolitan meal using French Boursin cheese, Italian Parmesan cheese, and Mexican tortillas.

No-stick cooking spray

3 ounces portobello mushrooms, sliced

3 ounces button mushrooms, sliced

2 garlic cloves, peeled and minced

1 medium onion, peeled and chopped

2 tablespoons red wine

8 ounces watercress

1 cup 2-percent milk

4 ounces low-fat Boursin cheese, softened

2 egg whites, beaten

1 whole large egg, beaten

3 large flour tortillas (made without lard)

2 tablespoons freshly grated Parmesan cheese

1. Preheat the oven to 400°F. Heat a saucepan over high heat for 30 seconds and spray it. Reduce the heat to medium.

2. Add the mushrooms, garlic, and onion to the pan and cook, stirring, until the vegetables soften and the onion turns translucent, about 5 minutes. Add the red wine and watercress and cook the watercress until wilted, about 2 minutes.

3. Meanwhile, in a bowl, mix the milk, Boursin cheese, and eggs together until smooth. Pour the watercress mixture into an oven-safe baking dish coated with the cooking spray and cover with the cheese mixture.

4. Bake for 30 to 35 minutes or until the custard is set. Spoon the custard into each tortilla and top with Parmesan cheese.

bodacious beverages and scintillating snacks

blue banana smoothie >>

nutrition info

For **2 servings** each serving contains:

Calories:	364
Fat:	1g
Protein:	13g
Cholesterol:	4mg
Carbohydrates:	81g
Sodium:	160mg

For **3 servings** each serving contains:

Calories:	243
Fat:	<1g
Protein:	9g
Cholesterol:	3mg
Carbohydrates:	54g
Sodium:	107mg

Yes, we have no blue bananas.

1 cup skim milk

1 cup plain nonfat yogurt

2 large overripe bananas

1 cup frozen blueberries

1½ teaspoons vanilla

1½ tablespoons honey

Combine all the ingredients in a blender and blend until smooth.

citrus tea >>

This is a satisfying way to benefit from the flavonoids and phenolics found in citrus fruits and the monoterpenes and limonene found in the citrus oil of the rind. This tea is also delicious when iced.

4 orange sections

¼ teaspoon grated orange rind

Juice of ¼ lemon

4 whole cloves

1-inch cinnamon stick

1 decaf tea bag (orange pekoe or black tea)

2 cups boiling water

Honey (optional)

1. Remove fibrous skin from the orange sections and break the sections into small pieces. Put into a tea pot. Add the orange rind, lemon juice, cloves, cinnamon stick, and tea bag.

2. Pour the boiling water into a teapot, cover, and steep for 5 minutes. Remove the tea bag. Pour through a strainer. Serve hot or iced with honey, if desired.

nutrition info

For **2 servings** each serving contains:

Calories:	32
Fat:	<1g
Protein:	<1g
Cholesterol:	0mg
Carbohydrates:	9g
Sodium:	7mg

For **3 servings** each serving contains:

Calories:	21
Fat:	<1g
Protein:	<1g
Cholesterol:	0mg
Carbohydrates:	6g
Sodium:	5mg

fruit punch >>

Here's an easy fruit punch recipe that everyone will enjoy.

nutrition info

For **2 servings** each serving contains:

Calories:	210
Fat:	<1g
Protein:	1g
Cholesterol:	0mg
Carbohydrates:	54g
Sodium:	33mg

For **3 servings** each serving contains:

Calories:	140
Fat:	<1g
Protein:	<1g
Cholesterol:	0mg
Carbohydrates:	36g
Sodium:	22mg

⅔ cup fresh lemon juice (about 4 lemons)

⅔ cup strawberries

1½ cups water

¾ cup apple juice concentrate

Place all the ingredients into a blender and puree until smooth.

island daiquiri >>

If you've never had guanabana juice, you're in for a treat. You can find it canned in the exotic fruits section of super-markets or in international food stores.

2 cups ice, cubed or crushed

Juice of 3 limes

5 tablespoons sugar

4 ounces guanabana juice

2 ripe peaches, peeled and sliced

1. Place the ice in a blender.

2. Mix together the lime juice and sugar. Pour it over the ice.

3. Rinse out any sugar mixture residue with the guanabana juice and pour this over the ice.

4. Place the peaches in the blender and blend until smooth.

nutrition info

*For **2 servings** each serving contains:*

Calories:	227
Fat:	<1g
Protein:	1g
Cholesterol:	0mg
Carbohydrates:	61g
Sodium:	13mg

*For **3 servings** each serving contains:*

Calories:	151
Fat:	<1g
Protein:	1g
Cholesterol:	0mg
Carbohydrates:	41g
Sodium:	9mg

lassi >>

Lassi is not a misspelling of the famous dog's name, it is a traditional Indian drink. Although this is not a traditional recipe, it is sooo refreshing.

1⅓ cups crushed ice

1 mango, peeled and sliced

⅔ cup buttermilk

2 strawberries

1 tablespoon honey

Combine all the ingredients in a blender and blend until smooth.

muscular
mocha >>

This tart high-calorie treat is a great instant meal in a pinch or an after–strength training nutrient replenisher. It stacks up well next to the commercial brands that contain approximately 520 calories, 25 grams of protein, 86 grams of carbohydrate, and 10 grams of fat in an equivalent portion size.

1 packet chocolate Carnation Instant Breakfast powder

1 cup low-fat coffee yogurt

1 cup skim milk

2 ice cubes, crushed

Place all the ingredients in a blender and process for 1 minute or until ice is blended. Drink immediately.

nutrition info

For **2 servings** each serving contains:

Calories:	442
Fat:	2g
Protein:	27g
Cholesterol:	19mg
Carbohydrates:	73g
Sodium:	523mg

For **3 servings** each serving contains:

Calories:	295
Fat:	1g
Protein:	18g
Cholesterol:	13mg
Carbohydrates:	49g
Sodium:	349mg

pineapple zing >>

The Sit-n-Spin, a great laundromat/rock-n-roll club in Seattle serves a drink similar to this one. The fresh ginger really gives it zing!

1 cup pineapple juice

½ cup peach nectar or juice

1 teaspoon minced fresh ginger

Place all the ingredients in a blender and blend for 30 seconds. Serve with or without ice.

nutrition info

For **2 servings** each serving contains:

Calories:	104
Fat:	<1g
Protein:	1g
Cholesterol:	0mg
Carbohydrates:	26g
Sodium:	6mg

For **3 servings** each serving contains:

Calories:	70
Fat:	<1g
Protein:	<1g
Cholesterol:	0mg
Carbohydrates:	17g
Sodium:	4mg

raspberry
lemongrass
iced tea >>

Monoterpenes, found in significant amounts in lemongrass, have been associated with a reduction in the risk of cancer of the breast, skin, liver, lung, stomach, and pancreas. We prefer fresh lemongrass to dried. To find fresh lemongrass, go to gourmet, international, or natural foods stores.

1 ounce fresh lemongrass

4 cups water

½ cup raspberries

1 to 2 tablespoons honey

1 teaspoon chopped fresh mint

1. Separate the lemongrass into individual layers. In a pot, bring the water and lemongrass to a boil. Reduce the heat to low and cook for 20 minutes.

2. Meanwhile, puree the raspberries in a food processor until smooth. Strain through a sieve to remove the seeds. Remove the lemongrass from the water and add the raspberries. Add the honey to taste and pour over ice. Garnish with the fresh mint.

nutrition info

*For **2 servings** each serving contains:*

Calories:	97
Fat:	<1g
Protein:	1g
Cholesterol:	0mg
Carbohydrates:	24g
Sodium:	24mg

*For **3 servings** each serving contains:*

Calories:	65
Fat:	<1g
Protein:	<1g
Cholesterol:	0mg
Carbohydrates:	16g
Sodium:	16mg

tropical shake >>

This Caribbean delight is to die for!

1 mango, peeled and diced

2 frozen bananas, peeled (see note)

1 cup 2-percent milk

½ teaspoon vanilla extract

Place all the ingredients in a blender and puree until smooth.

Note: Freeze bananas with the skins on and peel before using. They will take about 6 hours to freeze.

power balls >>

YIELD: ABOUT **16** BALLS

The homemade answer to Power Bars, these energy-packed treats will keep you carbo-charged, yet will temper any sugar rushes with a bit of protein and fat to slow down the absorption rate. Power Balls pack well and can be easily popped into your mouth while cycling, rowing, climbing, or hiking. Store them in an airtight container in a cool place and they will stay fresh for 2 weeks.

½ cup chopped dates

½ cup whole mission figs (destemmed)

½ cup raisins

¼ cup wheat germ

5 tablespoons nonfat dry milk powder

½ cup graham cracker crumbs

2 teaspoons fresh lemon juice

1. In a food processor, combine the dates, figs, raisins, wheat germ, and milk powder, and process until the mixture forms a ball. In a small bowl, mix the crumbs with the lemon juice.

2. Form the fruit mixture into 1-inch balls and roll in the crumbs to coat.

nutrition info

For **2 servings** each serving contains:

Calories:	484
Fat:	5g
Protein:	11g
Cholesterol:	2mg
Carbohydrates:	108g
Sodium:	248mg

For **3 servings** each serving contains:

Calories:	323
Fat:	3g
Protein:	7g
Cholesterol:	1mg
Carbohydrates:	72g
Sodium:	165mg

terrific trail mix >>

This version of trail mix will satisfy your chocolate craving and still meet your high-carb needs, without all the usual fat. It will store well for several weeks in an airtight container or resealable plastic bag in a cool place.

nutrition info

*For **2 servings** each serving contains:*

Calories:	440
Fat:	9g
Protein:	8g
Cholesterol:	0mg
Carbohydrates:	87g
Sodium:	211mg

*For **3 servings** each serving contains:*

Calories:	294
Fat:	6g
Protein:	5g
Cholesterol:	0mg
Carbohydrates:	58g
Sodium:	141mg

1 ounce semi-sweet chocolate chips (3 tablespoons)

1 ounce peanut butter chips (3 tablespoons)

2 ounces raisins (⅓ cup)

2⅓ cups Snack Wells Fat-Free Cinnamon Graham Snacks

1. On waxed paper, mix the chips together and melt in the microwave on high power for 2 minutes. Remove carefully from the microwave, taking care not to spill hot chocolate on yourself. Mix with a spatula and spread into a rectangular shape. Spread in the raisins and top with another piece of waxed paper. Press down to push raisins into the melted chocolate.

2. Freeze for 25 to 30 minutes to harden. Remove from the freezer and break up the candy into small chunks. Peel off waxed paper and place in a resealable plastic bag. Add grahams, mix, and enjoy.

CHAPTER TWELVE >>>

finale of fruits
and sweets

high performance
brownies >>

YIELD: **6 TO 8** SERVINGS

The secret here is the fruit butter—cutting the fat and spiking the carbs.

2 squares (2 ounces) unsweetened chocolate, melted

½ cup High Performance Fruit Butter (page 52) or prune butter (see note)

2 large eggs

1 cup sugar

1 teaspoon vanilla extract

½ cup unbleached all-purpose flour

⅛ teaspoon salt

No-stick cooking spray

1. Preheat the oven to 425°F.

2. Combine all the ingredients except the cooking spray, coat a 9-inch square baking pan with cooking spray, and pour in the batter.

3. Bake for 30 minutes.

Note: Prune butter is sold commercially as either prune butter or Lekvar.

cherry cheese
strudel >>

YIELD: **6 TO 8** SERVINGS

Austria is known for Mozart, The Sound of Music, *and the Alps. Yet it can be argued that strudel is Austria's finest contribution to the world community. And in this spirit we have created a low-fat strudel with cherries and orange zest, fruits that are high in monoterpenes.*

8 ounces nonfat ricotta cheese

1⅛ cups sugar

1 large egg

2 sheets phyllo dough

Butter-flavored no-stick cooking spray

½ teaspoon orange zest

½ pound fresh cherries, pitted (see note)

For 6 servings each serving contains:

Calories:	263
Fat:	6g
Protein:	6g
Cholesterol:	49mg
Carbohydrates:	48g
Sodium:	187mg

For 8 servings each serving contains:

Calories:	197
Fat:	4g
Protein:	5g
Cholesterol:	37mg
Carbohydrates:	36g
Sodium:	140mg

1. Preheat the oven to 400°F.

2. In a bowl, combine the ricotta cheese, ⅛ cup sugar, and egg and mix until blended. Set aside.

3. Place phyllo dough on a clean cloth. Spray dough evenly with the cooking spray and sprinkle evenly with the orange zest and ½ cup sugar. Place second sheet of phyllo on top.

4. Spoon the cheese filling in a straight line down one edge of the dough. Top the cheese with the cherries.

5. Using the cloth as a support, roll up the dough completely. Place it onto a cookie sheet. Spray the top of the strudel with the cooking spray and sprinkle it with the remaining sugar. Bake for 35 minutes.

Note: Unsweetened, frozen cherries may be substituted when fresh cherries are unavailable.

carrot cake >>

We have done it again. In our first book it was a rich, low-fat cheesecake. Now it is a healthful, low-fat carrot cake. Bravo!

nutrition info

For **6 servings** each serving contains:

Calories:	436
Fat:	16g
Protein:	6g
Cholesterol:	10mg
Carbohydrates:	70g
Sodium:	468mg

For **8 servings** each serving contains:

Calories:	327
Fat:	12g
Protein:	4g
Cholesterol:	7mg
Carbohydrates:	52g
Sodium:	351mg

1 cup grated carrots

1 cup unbleached all-purpose flour

1 cup sugar

1 teaspoon baking powder

1 teaspoon baking soda

1 teaspoon ground cinnamon

¼ teaspoon salt

⅓ cup chopped pecans

⅓ cup plus 1 tablespoon canola oil

3 egg whites, lightly beaten

No-stick cooking spray

cream cheese *glaze*

1 tablespoon skim milk

1 cup confectioner's sugar, sifted

1½ teaspoons fresh orange juice

⅓ cup Neufchâtel cheese (light cream cheese), softened

1. Preheat the oven to 325°F.

2. In a large bowl, combine the carrots, flour, sugar, baking powder, baking soda, cinnamon, salt, and pecans.

3. Add the oil to the dry ingredients, and mix until blended. Fold in the egg whites and mix thoroughly. Spray a 9-inch round pan and pour the batter into the pan.

4. Bake for 1 hour or until the cake springs back when touched. Cool completely.

5. To make the glaze, in a microwave-safe bowl, add 1 teaspoon of milk to the powdered sugar and mix until smooth. Repeat until all the milk has been added to sugar.

6. Add the orange juice to the mixture. Mix thoroughly and heat in the microwave for 30 seconds.

7. Blend in the Neufchâtel cheese and cool in the refrigerator until it is firm enough for glazing the cake.

8. Glaze the cake and allow it to set at least 30 minutes before serving.

citrus magic >>

This salad begins and ends with C: vitamin C, nature's perfect antioxidant.

nutrition info

For 2 servings each serving contains:

Calories:	181
Fat:	5g
Protein:	3g
Cholesterol:	0mg
Carbohydrates:	34g
Sodium:	1mg

For 3 servings each serving contains:

Calories:	121
Fat:	4g
Protein:	2g
Cholesterol:	0mg
Carbohydrates:	23g
Sodium:	<1mg

1 grapefruit, peeled and cubed

1 orange, peeled and cubed

1 tangerine, peeled and cubed

¼ cup chopped pecans

½ cup fresh orange juice

2 teaspoons sugar

1. Combine the fruit and pecans. Set aside.

2. Combine the orange juice with the sugar and mix. Pour over the fruit and serve.

dessert
dim sum >>

The key to these dumplings is the kasha. These buckwheat groats provide the nutty flavor in this sweet high-carb treat.

3½ tablespoons fresh orange juice

½ cup minus 1 tablespoon water

2 tablespoons finely ground kasha

Dash salt

2 pitted dried prunes, chopped

3 pitted dried apricots, chopped

1 tablespoon chopped dates

½ tablespoon honey

Pinch ground cinnamon

12 wonton wrappers

No-stick cooking spray

½ teaspoon confectioners' sugar

nutrition info

For **2 servings** each serving contains:

Calories:	231
Fat:	1g
Protein:	6g
Cholesterol:	4mg
Carbohydrates:	51g
Sodium:	278mg

For **3 servings** each serving contains:

Calories:	154
Fat:	<1g
Protein:	4g
Cholesterol:	3mg
Carbohydrates:	34g
Sodium:	185mg

1. Preheat the oven to 350°F. In a microwave-safe bowl, combine the orange juice, water, kasha, and salt. Microwave on medium for 6 minutes, or until the liquid is absorbed.

2. Combine the kasha with the prunes, apricots, dates, honey, and cinnamon and mix well. Place 1 teaspoon of the mixture in each wonton wrapper. Lightly wet the edges of each wrapper and pinch the corners together at the top to seal the dumpling.

3. Place the dumplings on a nonstick cookie sheet and spray dumplings lightly with cooking spray. Bake for 20 minutes, until slightly browned and crisp. Remove from the oven and sift the confectioners' sugar over the tops of dumplings. Serve warm or cold.

pump cake >>

YIELD: **6 TO 8** SERVINGS

This type of dessert was developed in the South. It was often called a "dump" cake. We prefer Pump Cake as it will pump you up with carbohydrates.

One 20-ounce can light cherry pie filling

One 9-ounce package chocolate cake mix

One 10-ounce can mandarin oranges, drained

5 tablespoons unsalted butter, slightly softened

1. Preheat the oven to 325°F.

2. Spread the cherry filling evenly over the bottom of a 9-inch square pan. Sprinkle the chocolate cake mix over cherries. Place the oranges on top.

3. Cut the butter into 25 thin slices; dot the fruit evenly with the butter slices.

4. Bake for 35 to 45 minutes or until the cake is done. Serve in the pan.

---

nutrition info

For **6 servings** each serving contains:

Calories:	326
Fat:	13g
Protein:	3g
Cholesterol:	16mg
Carbohydrates:	54g
Sodium:	420mg

For **8 servings** each serving contains:

Calories:	244
Fat:	10g
Protein:	3g
Cholesterol:	12mg
Carbohydrates:	40g
Sodium:	315mg

a honey of a honey cake >>

YIELD: **6 TO 8** SERVINGS

This spice cake packs well in backpacks and is a perfect trailside snack. It is loaded with carbs.

2¾ cups unbleached all-purpose flour

1 cup sugar

1 teaspoon baking powder

½ teaspoon ground cloves

½ teaspoon ground allspice

½ teaspoon ground cinnamon

1 large egg

4 large egg whites

8 ounces honey

¼ cup applesauce

1 teaspoon baking soda

1 cup cold coffee

¼ teaspoon vanilla

No-stick cooking spray

nutrition info

For **6 servings** *each serving contains:*

Calories:	486
Fat:	1g
Protein:	9g
Cholesterol:	31mg
Carbohydrates:	111g
Sodium:	342mg

For **8 servings** *each serving contains:*

Calories:	364
Fat:	1g
Protein:	7g
Cholesterol:	23mg
Carbohydrates:	84g
Sodium:	256mg

1. Preheat the oven to 350°F.

2. In a large bowl, combine the flour, sugar, baking powder, spices, egg, egg whites, honey, and applesauce. Mix thoroughly.

3. In another bowl, combine the baking soda and coffee and mix to dissolve. Pour the coffee mixture into the flour and stir until well beaten.

4. Spray a loaf pan and pour in the batter. Bake for 1 hour or until a toothpick comes out clean.

223

really rhubarb >>

Coaches often say that a team is greater than the individual players. This combination of strawberries and rhubarb makes a great team.

nutrition info

For **2 servings** each serving contains:

Calories:	262
Fat:	1g
Protein:	2g
Cholesterol:	0mg
Carbohydrates:	64g
Sodium:	5mg

For **3 servings** each serving contains:

Calories:	175
Fat:	<1g
Protein:	1g
Cholesterol:	0mg
Carbohydrates:	43g
Sodium:	5mg

8 ounces fresh or frozen rhubarb, chopped into 2-inch pieces

8 ounces strawberries, hulled and sliced

¼ cup water

½ cup sugar

1 teaspoon almond extract

1. In a saucepan, combine the rhubarb, strawberries, and water. Bring to a boil over high heat and immediately reduce the heat to low and cook for 20 minutes, or until the fruit is tender. Stir occasionally to prevent sticking.

2. Add the sugar and almond extract. Cook an additional 5 minutes. Serve chilled.

american rice pudding >>

YIELD: **4 TO 6** SERVINGS

Before the glut of fast-food restaurants cluttered America's landscape, diners were the heart and soul of roadside rural America. And it was in these diners that a legendary American classic was perfected. Our version features brown rice for added fiber.

2 cups 2-percent milk

½ cup instant brown rice

2 whole large eggs, separated

½ cup sugar

Dash salt

½ teaspoon vanilla

Golden raisins, optional

No-stick cooking spray

1. Preheat the oven to 350°F.

2. Cook the milk and rice in double boiler over simmering water for 20 to 30 minutes or until the rice is soft and tender. Stir occasionally.

3. In a medium bowl, beat the egg yolks. Add the sugar, salt, and vanilla. Add the rice, raisins, and any unabsorbed milk. Set aside.

4. In another bowl, beat the egg whites to the soft-peak stage and fold into the rice mixture.

5. Coat a 6-cup soufflé dish or ceramic bowl with the cooking spray. Place the dish or bowl inside a large roasting pan that has been filled halfway with water. Pour the rice mixture into the dish or bowl and bake for 30 minutes.

nutrition info

For **4 servings** each serving contains:

Calories:	277
Fat:	5g
Protein:	9g
Cholesterol:	103mg
Carbohydrates:	49g
Sodium:	90mg

For **6 servings** each serving contains:

Calories:	185
Fat:	3g
Protein:	6g
Cholesterol:	68mg
Carbohydrates:	33g
Sodium:	60mg

225

summer fruit
compote >>

nutrition info

For **6 servings** each serving contains:

Calories:	201
Fat:	1g
Protein:	2g
Cholesterol:	0mg
Carbohydrates:	51g
Sodium:	1mg

For **8 servings** each serving contains:

Calories:	151
Fat:	<1g
Protein:	1g
Cholesterol:	0mg
Carbohydrates:	38g
Sodium:	1mg

YIELD: **6 TO 8** SERVINGS

Even the king of compotes, Truman Compote, would have loved this heavenly summer dessert.

2 peaches

2 nectarines

4 sugar pears

6 Italian plums

1 cup water

¼ to ½ cup sugar

1. Core the fruit and cut it into ⅛-inch pieces, discarding the pits.

2. In a large saucepan, bring the water to a boil and add the fruit. Reduce the heat to low and cook the fruit for 20 minutes.

3. Add the sugar to taste and simmer an additional 10 minutes. Serve chilled.

key west sunset >>

YIELD: **4 TO 6** SERVINGS

Spontaneous applause follows sunsets on Key West. You'll also be clapping for this cool dessert that captures the colors of Key West's exploding sky.

For **4 servings** each serving contains:

Calories:	218
Fat:	5g
Protein:	2g
Cholesterol:	0mg
Carbohydrates:	47g
Sodium:	36mg

For **6 servings** each serving contains:

Calories:	145
Fat:	3g
Protein:	1g
Cholesterol:	0mg
Carbohydrates:	31g
Sodium:	24mg

1 small mango, peeled and pit removed and 1 small mango, peeled and cut into 1-inch pieces

1 tablespoon fresh lemon juice

1½ tablespoons honey

1 tablespoon Chambord (mixed berry liqueur)

1 pint fresh strawberries, hulled and quartered

½ small pineapple, peeled, cored, and cut into 1-inch pieces

1 kiwifruit, peeled and sliced

½ cup sweetened, shredded coconut, toasted (see note)

1. In a food processor or blender, puree the first mango with the lemon juice, honey, and Chambord until smooth. Set aside.

2. Place the strawberries, pineapple, second mango, and kiwifruit in a bowl. Toss with the mango sauce. Sprinkle with the toasted coconut and serve.

Note: Toast coconut in a dry skillet over medium-low heat for 5 to 8 minutes, stirring frequently and watching closely to prevent scorching.

fluffy sweet potato pie >>

For **6 servings** each serving contains:

Calories:	179
Fat:	9g
Protein:	3g
Cholesterol:	0mg
Carbohydrates:	21g
Sodium:	178mg

For **8 servings** each serving contains:

Calories:	134
Fat:	7g
Protein:	2g
Cholesterol:	0mg
Carbohydrates:	16g
Sodium:	134mg

YIELD: **6 TO 8** SERVINGS

The secret to our low-fat version of this Southern classic is the fluff.

crust

1⅓ cups unbleached, all-purpose flour

½ teaspoon salt

¼ cup vegetable oil

2½ tablespoons cold water

filling

1½ cups mashed cooked sweet potatoes

2 tablespoons unsalted butter, melted

½ cup brown sugar

¼ cup flour

½ cup marshmallow fluff

1 teaspoon fresh lemon juice

1 teaspoon grated orange zest

Pinch ground cinnamon

Pinch ground nutmeg

6 egg whites

1. Combine the flour, salt, and oil in a 9-inch pie pan. Mix until crumbly. Add the water 1 teaspoon at a time and mix until the dough is formed.

2. Pat the dough into the pie pan, handling it as little as possible. Preheat the oven to 325°F.

3. In a large bowl, combine all the filling ingredients except the egg whites, and beat until smooth. Set aside.

4. Beat the egg whites to the soft-peak stage and fold into the sweet potato mixture. Pour the mixture into the pie shell.

5. Bake for 1 hour.

bread pudding with
caramel sauce >>

For **4 servings** each serving contains:

Calories:	356
Fat:	8g
Protein:	12g
Cholesterol:	102mg
Carbohydrates:	61g
Sodium:	337mg

For **6 servings** each serving contains:

Calories:	237
Fat:	5g
Protein:	8g
Cholesterol:	68mg
Carbohydrates:	41g
Sodium:	225 mg

YIELD: **4 TO 6** SERVINGS

With such a great nutrient profile, you could eat this terrific dessert for breakfast and never feel guilty.

bread pudding

1 teaspoon unsalted butter

⅓ cup sugar

2 large eggs

Dash salt

1 teaspoon vanilla extract

2 cups 1-percent milk

8 slices raisin bread, cubed

caramel sauce

5 caramel candies (2 ounces total)

¼ cup skim milk

1. Preheat the oven to 400°F. Place the butter in the bottom of a loaf pan. Melt in the oven and coat the bottom of the pan.

2. In a bowl, combine the sugar, eggs, salt, vanilla, and milk, whisking until blended.

3. Place the bread in the pan and pour the egg mixture over it. Push down any pieces that are sticking up and are uncoated.

4. Bake for 30 minutes.

5. Meanwhile, to make the caramel sauce, combine the candy and milk in a microwave-safe dish. Heat on the medium setting in the microwave for 2 minutes, stirring every 30 seconds. After removing from the microwave stir until smooth. If the caramel is not completely melted, put it back into the microwave for an additional 10 to 20 seconds. Serve the bread pudding with the caramel sauce.

perfect parfait >>

Yes it's simple, but boy, it's good.

For **2 servings** *each serving contains:*

Calories:	403
Fat:	4g
Protein:	9g
Cholesterol:	7mg
Carbohydrates:	87g
Sodium:	127mg

For **3 servings** *each serving contains:*

Calories:	269
Fat:	3g
Protein:	6g
Cholesterol:	5mg
Carbohydrates:	58g
Sodium:	84mg

1 cup low-fat banana yogurt

½ cup low-fat granola

1 cup blueberries

1 cup low-fat peach yogurt

1 cup sliced strawberries

1 cup raspberries

1. Place 1 heaping tablespoonful of the banana yogurt at the bottom of each tall glass. Sprinkle with granola.

2. Layer the blueberries on top of the granola.

3. Place 1 heaping tablespoonful of the peach yogurt on top of the blueberries. Sprinkle with more granola.

4. Layer the strawberries on top of the granola.

5. Place the rest of the banana yogurt on the strawberries. Sprinkle with more granola.

6. Layer the raspberries on top of the yogurt and cover them with the remaining peach yogurt and granola.

Index